W9-DIW-206

Success in Writing

Writing to Describe

GLOBE FEARON
Pearson Learning Group

Executive Editor: Barbara Levadi
Senior Editor: Francie Holder
Project Editors: Karen Bernhaut, Douglas Falk, Amy Jolin
Editorial Assistant: Kris Shepos-Salvatore
Editorial Development: Kraft & Kraft
Production Director: Penny Gibson
Production Editor: Alan Dalgleish
Interior Design and Electronic Page Production: Blue Inc.
Marketing Manager: Nancy Surridge
Cover Design: Leslie Baker, Pat Smythe

ISBN 0-835-91891-2
Printed in the United States of America

7 8 9 10 11 12 13 14 15   05 04 03

1-800-321-3106
www.pearsonlearning.com

CONTENTS

UNIT 1 Understanding Description

Descriptive writing paints a picture in words. When you write a descriptive essay, your goal is to describe a person, place, or thing so clearly that it comes to life for your reader.

What to Do

Use description to share your own vision with your readers. There is no limit to possible topics when you write description. You might describe a friend, family member, classmate, or a stranger sitting across the room. You might describe your room at home or a planet you've seen only in your imagination. You might describe a pet, a shirt, a painting, or a building. You can describe whatever you feel the urge to write about.

Consider these goals when you write description:

- Give the reader a clear idea of what you're describing.
- Help the reader experience what you're describing

How to Do It

Follow these guidelines when you write description:

- Make a list of possible topics.
- Decide what you want to describe.
- Close your eyes and form a picture of your topic.
- Focus on a special part of what you want to describe. For example: "The most pleading eyes in the world belong to my dog when he's sitting by our dinner table."
- Think of details that will jump out at your reader. For example: "pleading eyes," "floppy ears," "droopy snout."
- Use vivid words to describe details. A "ferocious" dog is easier for a reader to picture than a "bad" dog.
- Keep in mind that description can be used as a part of other kinds of essays: persuasive, expository, or narrative.

Apply It

▶ Take a look around the room you are sitting in right now. Think about the things in it that you could describe. Then visualize another place. Think about describing something or someone there. Keep a list of these possible topics in your notebook.

CHAPTER 1 Building a Description

In a description, you can create images with words. The right words can make sights, sounds, smells, tastes, and feelings spring to life for your reader. No magic potions or formulas are necessary—just a few tips about how to create the right combination of words.

What to Do

Give your description a solid structure. Begin with a short introduction that shows the overall picture. Make your readers want to find out more about your topic. Then develop the body of your description with details in a clear order. Conclude with an image that will stay with your readers.

How to Do It

Keep this chart in mind. Here is what to do in each of the three parts of a descriptive essay.

> **INTRODUCTION**
> (1 paragraph)
>
> Get your reader's attention.
> Tell what you are going to describe.
> State your impression of your topic.

> **BODY**
> (1 or more paragraphs)
> Include sensory details to bring your topic to life.
> Arrange these details in a clear order.

> **CONCLUSION**
> (1 paragraph)
> Restate your impression.
> End with an image that will stay with your reader.

Review It

▶ Identify the three parts of a descriptive essay.

_____

_____

_____

Lesson 1 Making an Impression in the Introduction

You may have heard the old saying "First impressions are important." For your descriptive essay, the introduction is your reader's first impression. Like the opening scene of a movie, it's your chance to "hook" your audience so that they will want to see what comes next.

What to Do

If your introduction does three jobs, it will be a strong foundation for the rest of your description. This chart lists the three jobs that an introduction should do.

> **INTRODUCTION**
>
> (1 paragraph)
> Get your reader's attention.
> Tell what you are going to describe.
> State your impression of your topic.

How to Do It

Look at this example. It comes from a description a student named Hank wrote for the school newspaper.

> When was the last time you smiled at someone you passed on the street? Here in New York, people walk by quickly, with their heads down. They have their minds on business. They rarely stop to smile or say hello. Then the annual Third Avenue Street Fair arrives. It is a summertime carnival of ethnic food, upbeat music, and good feelings. People relax and slow down. They remember how to smile and say hello. For one day at least, the fair teaches people how to be friendly again!

Review It

1. Which sentence grabs the reader's attention?

_____

2. What is the topic of Hank's description?

_____

3. Which sentence states Hank's impression of the topic?

_____

Lesson 2 Providing Details in the Body

Once you have completed the introduction, you can move on to the body of your essay. This is where you develop the main part of your description.

What to Do

Choose the best way to organize your essay.

Spatial order, or order in space, is usually the best way to organize a descriptive essay. You can start at any point. Then your description can move from bottom to top, from left to right, from far to near, or from near to far.

How to Do It

Look at these sketches. They show two ways to organize the details of your description.

FAR TO NEAR (ZOOM IN)

Start by describing the whole scene.

Next, begin to focus on the most important part of the scene.

Finally, "zoom in" for a close-up of the important element.

NEAR TO FAR (ZOOM OUT)

Start by describing the most important element.

Next, describe what surrounds that element.

Finally, "zoom out" for a view of the whole scene.

Review It

▶ Look at the far-to-near series of pictures.

1. Write a sentence to describe the scene in the first picture.

_____

_____

2. Write a sentence to describe the scene in the second picture.

_____

_____

3. Write a sentence to describe the scene in the third picture.

_____

_____

▶ Here is part of an essay written by a student named Annie. She chose to organize her description from far to near.

I looked out at the audience at this year's prize assembly. I could feel my knees shaking. The auditorium was full. All those faces were looking at me, waiting for me to speak. When my eyes got used to the glare of the lights, I spotted my parents a few rows back. Dad was in his best gray suit and his striped tie. He was fiddling with his new camera. Next to him, my mom smiled proudly. In the front row was Mrs. Jilson, the principal. Next to her sat—gulp!—Governor Ellwood. He looked younger and thinner than he does on TV. He calmly studied the notes for his own speech. He had no idea how nervous he was making me.

4. What is the whole scene that Annie begins with?

_____

5. What is the last and smallest detail that Annie zooms in on?

_____

Lesson 3 Ending with a Strong Image

The conclusion of a descriptive essay should be like the closing scene of a movie. It should leave your audience with a strong image of your subject.

What to Do Conclude your essay with an image or picture that will stay in your reader's mind.

How to Do It The following conclusion is part of an essay written by a student named Diego. It is about a visit to his grandmother's in Puerto Rico.

> The ten days were over. I hated to leave my winter paradise. I walked across the sand to take one last look at the ocean in the light of the setting sun. I could see the blue-green bay. I could hear the waves lapping on the shore. I filled my hands with salt water and splashed it against my face. I tasted the salt on my tongue. For the last time I breathed in the warm tropical breeze. When I started walking toward the waiting van, seagulls circled overhead and squawked a sad good-bye.

Review It

1. What is the main impression the reader gets from this conclusion?

_____

_____

2. How do you think the writer feels about his vacation?

_____

3. What key words or details does the writer use to show this feeling?

_____

_____

4. In the margins, add some words or phrases of your own to the paragraph to create an even stronger image.

CHAPTER 2 Describing with Style

Sensory details, words that convey a mood, and vivid language help make your descriptive writing come to life. Sensory details are details that appeal to the senses. Words that convey a mood show your feelings. Vivid language gives readers a clear picture of what you are describing.

What to Do

Use description to make your writing come to life for your readers. In this chapter you will learn three ways to make your style effective:

- Using Your Senses
- Creating a Mood
- Using Vivid Language

How to Do It

Make your readers feel that they are experiencing what you experience. Use details that appeal to the five senses. The five senses are sight, smell, hearing, touch, and taste.

> The **dark** room, lighted only by **a flickering candle**, smelled of **dried flowers** and **old musty photographs**.

Create a mood that reflects your feelings about the subject. Use words and phrases that show emotion.

> When I remember my puppy, I remember his **hopeful face** and the **eager wag** of his **short tail**.

Use precise words and comparisons to bring your description into clear focus.

> The **terrified** child **clung like a stamp** to her mother. A neon sign above them **buzzed and flickered**. The woman **rushed** along in **pointy red shoes**.

Apply It

▶ Find examples of descriptive styles. Good places to look include literature anthologies, magazines, and brochures. Keep your examples in your notebook. Notice how the descriptions appeal to readers. If possible, discuss them with a partner or in a group.

Lesson 1   Using Your Senses

The key to a vivid description is in the details. Imagine a blurry black-and-white photograph. Then imagine the same photograph snapping into focus. Suddenly you can see all the details. It's the same with descriptive writing. The details make the subject snap into focus.

What to Do   Use your senses. Sensory details are the words and phrases that appeal to the senses. They will make your description come to life for your readers. The best way of adding details to your description is to use your senses of sight, smell, hearing, touch, and taste.

How to Do It   This sensory details web shows how Diego used all five senses in the paragraph on page 10.

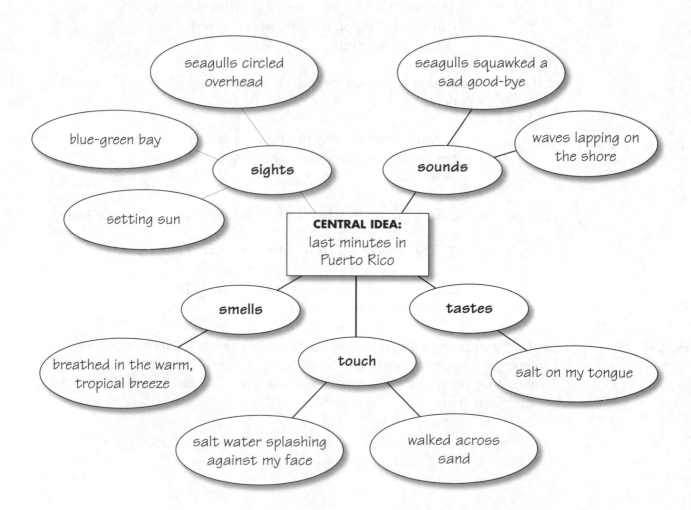

Apply It ▶ Practice using details in your description. Fill in this sensory details web. Look around you. What do you see, hear, taste, smell, and feel? Use all five senses to fill the web.

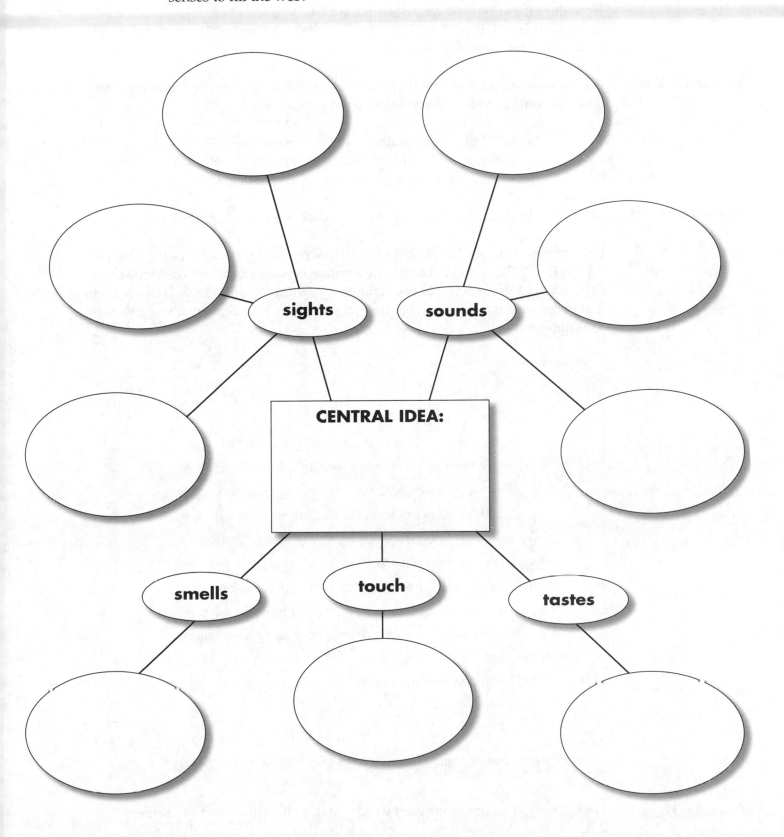

Lesson 2 Creating a Mood

How does the subject of your description make you feel? When you include your feelings about what you're describing, you establish a mood. You can make your readers feel the same way you do.

What to Do   Decide what mood you want to convey in your description. The following words describe some moods that you might want to convey:

> horror pleasure calm worry friendliness loneliness
> comfort discomfort satisfaction disappointment
> annoyance happiness joy sorrow

How to Do It   After you choose a mood, choose words and details that support that mood.

Look at this example. Remember Diego's description on page 10 of the beach in Puerto Rico? The mood of Diego's description was pleasant. You could tell that he liked being at the beach. You could tell that he didn't want to leave. Here is a letter that his sister Carmen sent to her best friend at home. It seems that she saw things a bit differently.

Dear Michele,

   I am sitting on a deck chair looking out on the same boring scene I have seen every day for a week. There is a small bay with waves just big and loud enough to keep me up at night. I hear the seagulls squawking. They squawk all day long. Right now I'm slapping at my other favorite flying pests—mosquitoes the size of ping-pong balls. I have spent most of the vacation scratching. I don't know whether the itch comes from mosquito bites or my peeling sunburn. It will take weeks to wash the sand and salt out of my hair.

   See you in one more week,
   Carmen

Review It   1. In What to Do, underline each word that describes the mood of Carmen's letter.
2. Underline words and phrases in her letter that help to create the mood you identified in question 1.

Lesson 3 Using Vivid Language

You've learned how to use details to get your description to snap into focus like a sharp photograph. Now imagine a black-and-white photograph suddenly blooming into full color. That's what can happen to your essay if you use vivid language to describe details.

What to Do   Use vivid details. Here are three characteristics of a vivid detail:
- It is specific, not general.
- It appeals to at least one of the five senses.
- It is complete. No important piece of information is missing.

How to Do It   Look at the details listed below. The details in the left column are not vivid. They are general, they do not appeal to the senses, and they do not give full information. The details in the right column are specific, sensory, and complete.

VAGUE	VIVID
bird	squawking seagull
car	gleaming red convertible
sandwich	rare hamburger with melted Swiss cheese
building	shining skyscraper in the golden sunset

Review It   ▶ Revise the following descriptive paragraph. Replace the underlined details with more vivid ones. Make your changes right on the page.

My new stereo has <u>amazing</u> speakers. They are painted <u>black</u>. The front is covered with <u>cloth</u>. High notes <u>sound good</u>. The bass notes are <u>really amazing</u>. When I turn the volume up, they are <u>loud</u>. At low volume they <u>sound nice</u>.

Apply It   ▶ Choose one of the topics in your notebook to describe. Jot down details about the topic. Make them vivid.

What Have You Learned in Unit 1?

Use these questions to gather and review your thoughts about the importance of each key point in Unit 1. Don't worry about writing complete sentences. Just put some thoughts, ideas, and reactions down for each.

1. What is descriptive writing?

_____

2. What should an introduction to a descriptive essay contain?

_____

3. What should you include in the body of a descriptive essay?

_____

4. What are two ways to order the details in the body of a descriptive essay?

_____

5. How should you conclude a descriptive essay?

_____

6. Why would you use sensory details in a description?

_____

7. What do sensory details appeal to?

_____

8. What is meant by the mood of an essay?

_____

9. What mood or impression do you hope to convey in a descriptive essay?

_____

10. What can you do to improve words and phrases in a description?

_____

UNIT 2 Writing to Describe

A cross-town hike may seem like more than you can handle when you first think about doing it. If you take one step at a time, you will be there before you know it. Writing an essay is like that. If you break it into steps, each step will seem easier.

What to Do Follow three basic steps when you write to describe. In this unit, you will learn the three basic steps.

- Planning Your Writing
- Developing Your Writing
- Completing Your Writing

How to Do It Keep this outline in mind. It shows the smaller steps within the three larger ones.

Plan your writing.

Choose a topic.
Narrow the topic.
Identify the audience.
Identify the purpose.
Gather details.
Organize your description.

Develop your writing.

Draft the introduction.
Draft the body.
Draft the conclusion.

Complete your writing.

Revise your essay.
Proofread your essay.
Publish your essay.

Apply It ▶ Imagine yourself writing description. Begin by looking for examples of descriptive writing in the everyday world. You may already have examples in your notebook from your work on page 11. If not, look in brochures, magazines, newspapers, journals, novels, and textbooks. Visualize yourself going through each step. If you can, discuss the steps with a partner or group.

CHAPTER 1 Planning Your Writing

Plan what you want to say. Plan how to say it. You will have a much better chance of writing a vivid description if you do.

What to Do

Get your writing off to a good start. When does the writing of a description start? Is it when you start a draft? No, it is earlier than that. Is it when you first make some notes? No, it is even earlier than that. Writing begins as soon as you start thinking about your topic.

Many of your first ideas will appear in the final draft of your writing. Taking the time to think and plan at the start will make that final draft as good as it can be.

How to Do It

Follow this checklist. In this chapter, you will work through all the steps that are needed to plan a descriptive essay. They are listed in this checklist.

☐ Start by choosing a topic that is familiar to you. Your essay will be strongest if you collect a few ideas for topics, then choose the best one. Use an idea branch. List topics in your notebook.

☐ Once you have chosen your topic, narrow it until it fits your assignment and the space and time available to you. Use a topic web.

☐ Think about the people who will read your finished essay. You must make sure that they understand what you are saying. Complete audience profile forms.

☐ Decide what your purpose for writing is. The basic purpose of a descriptive essay is to show your audience how your topic looks, sounds, feels, tastes, and smells.

☐ Gather the details you need to bring your description to life. Use details that appeal to the five senses.

☐ Organize your details so that your reader will understand them.

Apply It

▶ As you complete the lessons in this chapter, return to this page to check off each step. You will be able to see the progress you are making.

Lesson 1　Choosing a Topic

The best descriptive essays are about subjects that you know well. When you choose a topic that is familiar to you, you can bring it to life for your readers.

What to Do

Think about the things you enjoy talking about. You might think of your favorite foods, a concert you heard, or a great play you made in a game. Let your thoughts and ideas flow. Let one thought lead you to another.

How to Do It

Use an idea branch to explore your ideas. Here's how a student named Chandler followed his thoughts about his favorite sport, baseball.

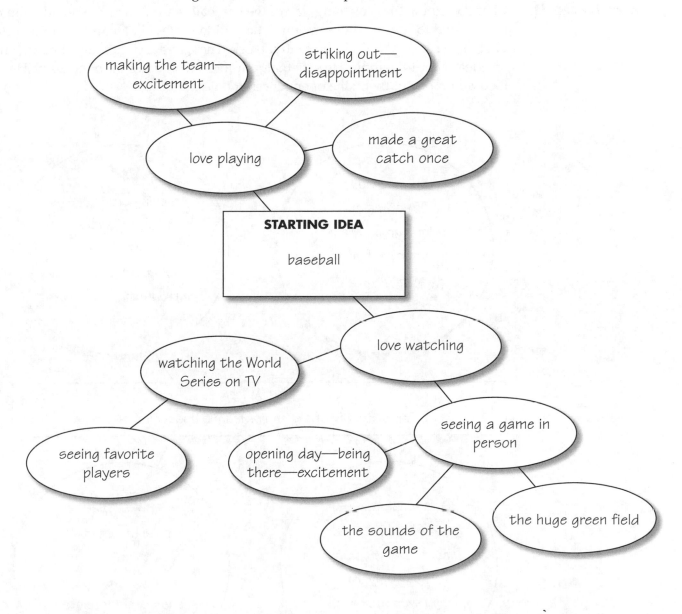

Apply It

▶ On a separate piece of paper, make your own idea branch to explore topics. Let your thoughts wander as ideas come to you. Put check marks next to the ideas that appeal to you.

Lesson 2 Narrowing a Topic

Once you have chosen a topic, you may have to narrow it. Make the topic narrow enough to cover in a short essay.

What to Do

Think about what you want to describe. Is it too broad for a short essay? Is there too much information to cover in four or five paragraphs? Suppose you wanted to describe the first day of a new school year. You would have too much to tell. The topic is too broad. You would have to narrow it. You could focus on one part of the day.

How to Do It

Chandler knew that "opening day of the baseball season" was too broad a topic. He decided to narrow it to something he could work with. He used a topic web. First, he wrote his topic in the central block. Then, in the circles, he jotted down his ideas about the topic. He saw that four ideas would not fit in his essay. He focused on one of them: the opening ceremonies.

the stadium:
fresh paint
bright green grass
banners flying
new scoreboard

✔
opening ceremonies:
national anthem
fireworks
throwing out the first ball
introducing old-timers
"play ball!"

CENTRAL IDEA
opening day of the major league baseball season

the players:
nervous rookies
confident veterans
star players
my favorite players

the crowd:
colorful outfits
banners
mixed ages
cheers and chants

Apply It

▶ Use this web to narrow your topic. Write your topic in the central block. Write your ideas in the circles.

▶ Decide which idea you feel most strongly about. Choose that one to develop into your essay.

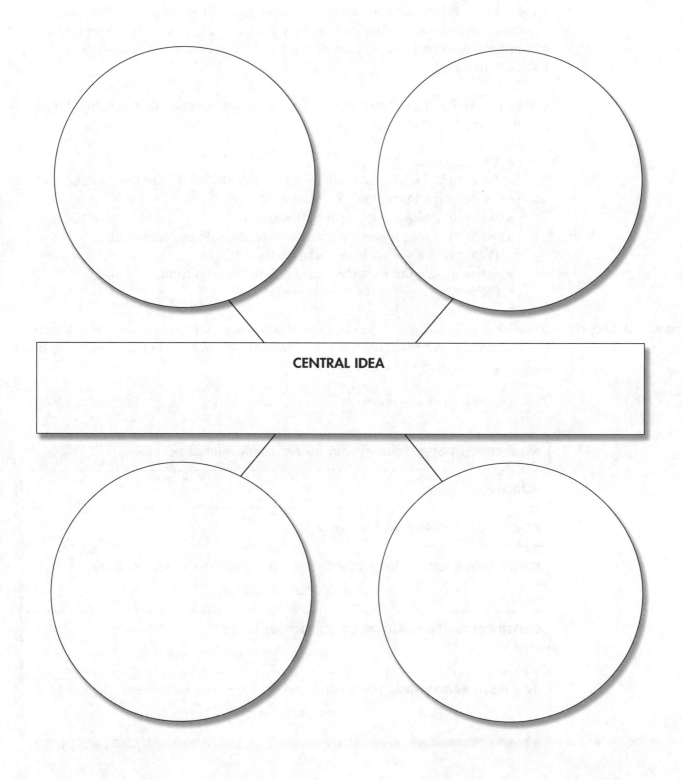

CENTRAL IDEA

Lesson 3   Identifying the Audience

Your audience is your readers. Your audience may include your teacher, parents, classmates, and anyone else you plan to share your work with.

What to Do

Think about your audience. How much do you need to describe to bring your subject to life for them? For example, to most Americans the phrase "baseball diamond" calls up a familiar picture. However, that phrase would mean nothing to someone who had never heard of baseball. You would have to describe a baseball diamond.

Before you write, think about who your readers are. Decide the following things about them:

- their ages and positions
  (Are they classmates or are they younger students? Are they adults, such as the school principal or a teacher?)
- what they already know about your topic
- what they might need to know to understand your topic fully
  (What will you *have to* describe for them?)
- what special interests they have regarding your topic
  (What will they *want* you to describe?)

How to Do It

Make an audience profile. Before Chandler began to write his essay, he took some time to think about his audience. He knew that he wanted to read his essay to his classmates. He made an audience profile for them.

This is the profile he made:

NARROWED TOPIC: opening day at a major-league game
AUDIENCE: classmates
AGE RANGE/POSITION: teenagers/students
KNOWLEDGE REGARDING TOPIC: They have probably all watched or even played baseball.
OTHER FACTS THEY MAY NEED TO KNOW: They may not know what is special about opening day.
INTERESTS REGARDING TOPIC: They may not feel the excitement. I'll have to communicate it to them.

Apply It   ▶ Think of possible audiences for your descriptive essay. Choose two possible audiences. Use the following forms to make a profile for each one.

NARROWED TOPIC:
AUDIENCE:
AGE RANGE/POSITION:
KNOWLEDGE REGARDING TOPIC:
OTHER FACTS THEY MAY NEED TO KNOW:
INTERESTS REGARDING TOPIC:

NARROWED TOPIC:
AUDIENCE:
AGE RANGE/POSITION:
KNOWLEDGE REGARDING TOPIC:
OTHER FACTS THEY MAY NEED TO KNOW:
INTERESTS REGARDING TOPIC:

▶ When you have finished your profiles, work with a partner if you can. Talk about the audiences you have profiled. Decide which one you would most like to reach. Choose that one audience for your descriptive essay.

Lesson 4 Identifying the Purpose

The purpose of an essay is the reason it is written. The purpose of a descriptive essay is to show the audience how the topic looks, sounds, smells, tastes, and feels.

What to Do

Ask yourself how you can make your readers experience what you are describing. You want it to be as vivid and real for them as it is for you.

Do you want to give a neutral, or plain, description of your topic? Or do you want to include your feelings in your description? Both of these are good ways to describe. You should choose the approach that appeals to you more.

How to Do It

Compare these two drafts that Chandler wrote. The one on the left is neutral. Chandler's purpose was to describe his baseball glove. The one on the right includes Chandler's feelings. His purpose was to show that he likes the glove.

My baseball glove is there on the shelf in its usual place. When it was new, it was stiff and bright yellow. Now it is brown and soft with age and use. I take it down and pound my fist in the blackened pocket. I hear the familiar "thwack." The smell of leather is mixed with the smell of grass.

It is a pleasure to see my baseball glove on the shelf in its usual place. I remember how stiff it was when it was new. I like it much better now that it's soft and brown from years of hard play. I take it down and pound my fist in the blackened pocket. I hear the satisfying "thwack." It reminds me of long fly balls I've caught. The smell of leather is mixed with the smell of grass. All of it reminds me of great moments spent playing ball.

Review It

▶ Underline the details in the paragraph on the right that show the writer's feelings.

Apply It

▶ Decide which method serves your purpose better: a neutral description or one that includes your feelings. Keep that method in mind when you write your essay.

Lesson 5 Gathering Sensory Details

You can gather details by using your five senses. These details are called sensory details. To recall sensory details, you may have to question yourself the way a detective questions a witness. Ask yourself what you saw, heard, felt, smelled, and tasted.

What to Do   Use your five senses to gather information for your descriptive essay. The five senses are touch, sight, smell, taste, and hearing. A good description might emphasize one sense over the others. You may not have any details for one or two senses. Try to include as many sensory details as you can.

How to Do It   This is the sensory details web that Chandler used for the description of his baseball glove. Notice that he had no details for taste.

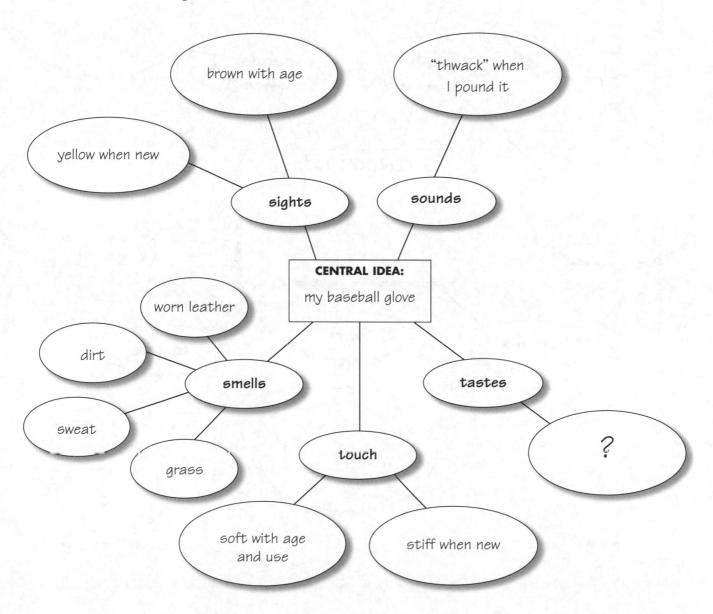

Apply It   ▶ Complete the following sensory details web for your topic.

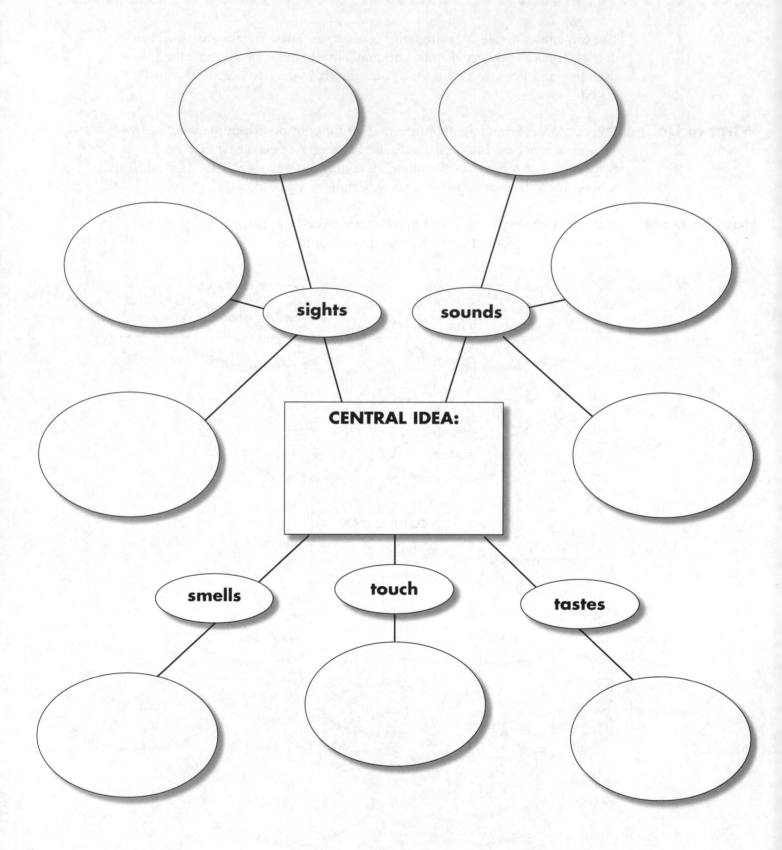

sights

sounds

CENTRAL IDEA:

smells

touch

tastes

Lesson 6 Organizing Details

You have gathered the information for your descriptive essay. Now you need to give shape and form to this information.

What to Do

Organize your details. If you just write the details as you think of them, you will have a list, not an essay. Organize your details so that your readers can understand them. Here are two ways to organize a description:

METHOD	BEST USES	WAYS TO PRESENT DETAILS
SPATIAL ORDER	• to give an overall picture • to show how parts are related	• from side to side • from near to far • from far to near
ORDER OF IMPORTANCE	• to emphasize the most important details	• from most important to least important • from least important to most important

How to Do It

Compare these two drafts that Chandler wrote. The one on the left uses spatial order. The one on the right uses order of importance.

I stepped up to the plate. I peered out at my opponents on the field. To my left was Freddy McGuane, the third baseman. He was a giant. I couldn't imagine hitting anything past him. Directly ahead of me was the best player on their team, Orlando Ruiz, the pitcher. He was tall and lanky. He had a blazing fastball. I would be lucky to hit anything he threw. To my right, playing first base, was Dahong Park. He was a great slugger, but not a good fielder.

I stepped up to the plate. I peered out at my opponents on the field. To my right, playing first base, was Dahong Park. He was a great slugger, but not a good fielder. To my left was Freddy McGuane, the third baseman. He was a giant. I couldn't imagine hitting anything past him. Directly ahead of me was the best player on their team, Orlando Ruiz, the pitcher. He was tall and lanky. He had a blazing fastball. I would be lucky to hit anything he threw.

Apply It

▶ Begin to organize your descriptive essay. Decide which method you want to use. List your details in that order.

CHAPTER 2 Developing Your Writing

As you write your drafts, work from your plan. Keep your audience and purpose in mind. Make your writing do its job.

What to Do

Get your ideas on paper.

Each version of your writing is called a draft. To get the first draft on paper, start writing wherever it is easiest for you to begin. For example, you might want to start by copying a sentence from your notes. Let your ideas flow from there. Do not worry about spelling or grammar right now.

How to Do It

Follow this checklist. In this chapter, you will work through all the steps that are needed to develop a descriptive essay. They are listed in this checklist.

☐ Draft the introduction. Get your essay off to a good start. Grab the reader's attention with a strong statement or question. Be sure to mention your topic. Give the reader an overall impression of it.

☐ Draft the body. You identified your topic and gave a general view of it in the introduction. Now describe it in detail in the body of your essay. Use sensory details. These are details that appeal to the five senses. The five senses are sight, hearing, touch, taste, and smell.

☐ Draft the conclusion. Like your introduction, your conclusion should give a general view of the topic. Bring your reader back to the big picture. If it suits your purpose, tell them your feelings about the topic. End with a strong image that your readers will remember.

Apply It

▶ As you complete the lessons in this chapter, return to this page to check off each step. You will be able to see the progress you are making.

Lesson 1 Drafting the Introduction

Get your essay off to a good start. Grab the reader's attention with a strong statement or question.

What to Do

Follow these hints:

- Use your notes as a guide as you write.
- Start with a sentence that will grab the readers' interest.
    - Turn your topic sentence into a surprising question.
    - Pick one outstanding detail. Write a strong statement or question about it.
- Identify your topic.
- In one sentence, give the reader a general impression of the topic.
- If you are not sure how to give a strong general impression, just do the best you can. Later, after you have written the body, you can look back and make changes.
- Do not worry about spelling and grammar right now. You will have time to edit your work later.
- If you get stuck, save the introduction for later. Go on to the next lesson. Begin to draft the body of your essay. Once the body is finished, the introduction may be easier to write.

How to Do It

Look at this example. Chandler wanted to write about opening day at Yankee Stadium. He wrote a sentence to grab the readers' interest.

First, he started with his topic statement.

Then he turned it into a question.

Finally, he made the question more surprising.

> When I go to Yankee Stadium I can imagine the great players of the past.
>
> Have you ever imagined the great players who played at Yankee Stadium?
>
> Have you ever seen the ghosts who haunt Yankee Stadium?

He began his introduction with this sentence.

He gave a general view of his topic.

> Have you ever seen the ghosts who haunt Yankee Stadium? Sometimes I think I have. I was in the crowd on opening day. When I looked out at the field, I imagined that I saw the great players of the past out there.

Apply It

▶ On a separate sheet of paper, draft the introduction to your essay. Look at your sensory details web on page 26. Find a detail that will grab the readers' attention. Start your introduction with a sentence about that detail.

Lesson 2 Drafting the Body

You gave a general view of your topic in the introduction. In the body of your essay, you will describe it in detail. Use details that appeal to the five senses. The five senses are sight, hearing, touch, taste, and smell.

What to Do

Follow these hints:

- Use your notes as a guide as you write.
- Present your details in the order that you decided upon on page 27. Save a strong image for the conclusion.
- If you are not sure that the order you chose is really the right order for your topic, follow your plan for now. Later, you can revise the body of your essay and move sentences around.
- As you write, keep your audience and purpose firmly in mind. Think about what your readers know about your topic. Think about what they need to know.
- Do not worry about spelling and grammar right now. Just get your sensory details on paper! You will have time to revise and proofread later.

How to Do It

Study this example. This is the draft of the body of Chandler's essay.

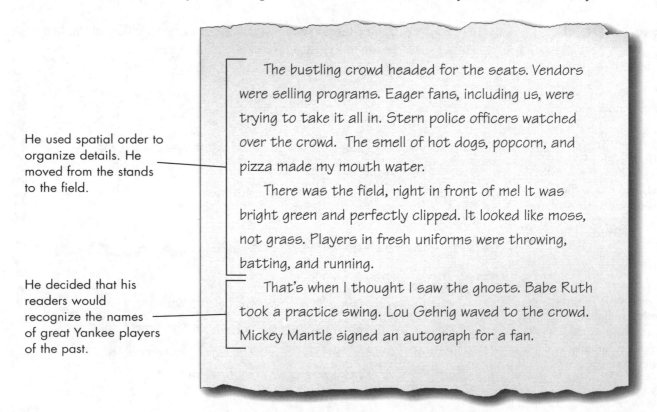

He used spatial order to organize details. He moved from the stands to the field.

The bustling crowd headed for the seats. Vendors were selling programs. Eager fans, including us, were trying to take it all in. Stern police officers watched over the crowd. The smell of hot dogs, popcorn, and pizza made my mouth water.

There was the field, right in front of me! It was bright green and perfectly clipped. It looked like moss, not grass. Players in fresh uniforms were throwing, batting, and running.

He decided that his readers would recognize the names of great Yankee players of the past.

That's when I thought I saw the ghosts. Babe Ruth took a practice swing. Lou Gehrig waved to the crowd. Mickey Mantle signed an autograph for a fan.

Apply It

▶ On a separate sheet of paper, draft the body of your essay. Use the notes that you took on page 26. Use the organization you chose on page 27.

Lesson 3 Drafting the Conclusion

Your conclusion should take your readers back to a large view of the topic. You may want to sum up your feelings about the topic. Leave them with an image that they will remember.

What to Do   Follow these hints:

- Use your notes as a guide as you write.
- Restate your overall picture of the topic. Look back at the introduction. Rephrase the sentence you used there to grab your readers' attention. Add something more to it.
- Add a sentence about your feelings, if you want to.
- End with an image that your readers will remember. Pick one detail that stands out. Write a sentence about it.
- Do not worry about spelling and grammar right now. Focus on writing a strong conclusion to your essay. You will have time to correct any errors later.
- If you have trouble writing the conclusion, go back and work on the introduction some more. The introduction and the conclusion work together. The introduction opens your description. The conclusion closes it. Go back and forth between them. You will find that one gives you ideas for the other.

How to Do It   Look at this example. The first paragraph is Chandler's introduction. The second is his conclusion. Notice how they work together.

> Have you ever seen the ghosts who haunt Yankee Stadium? Sometimes I think I have. I was in the crowd on opening day. When I looked out at the field I imagined that I saw the great players of the past out there.

> The national anthem came over the speaker system. When it ended, the whole stadium seemed to hold its breath for a moment. "Play ball!" shouted the umpire. The ghosts vanished, and the game began.

Apply It   ▶ On a separate sheet of paper, write a draft of the conclusion to your essay. Use your introduction to gather ideas.

CHAPTER 3 Completing Your Writing

When the first draft is written, return to it to make it better. Revise it to make it stronger. Proofread it to make it correct. Then publish it to bring it to your audience.

What to Do

Make your writing better with every draft. Revise the first draft to make a second draft that is better.

Keep working at your drafts until your writing says just what you want it to say as well as you can say it. Draft, revise, and revise again until you are pleased with your work.

How to Do It

Follow this checklist. In this chapter, you will work through all the steps that are needed to complete a descriptive essay. They are listed in this checklist.

☐ Revise your essay. You have your description down on paper. Now it is time to go back and revise. Read your draft carefully. Make changes to be sure that you described your subject clearly. Use the revision checklist on page 34 to correct and strengthen your writing.

☐ Proofread your essay. Fix any mistakes in spelling, grammar, and punctuation. Read your revised draft sentence by sentence and word by word. Look for the little mistakes that you might have missed or ignored earlier. Use the proofreading checklist on page 35 to find and correct any mistakes.

☐ Publish your essay to bring it to your audience. Find the best way to reach your audience. Follow the requirements of the publishing method you choose.

Apply It

▶ As you complete the lessons in this chapter, return to this page to check off each step. You will be able to see the progress you are making.

Lesson 1 Revising Your Essay

Revising means changing your work to make it even better. A good way to find out where your essay needs improvement is to ask a friend to read it.

What to Do   Make improvements in your work.

Start by reading what you have written. Don't make changes now. Just read.

Then read your work again. This time, begin making changes. Use the revision checklist on the next page to guide your work. Keep making changes until your writing says just what you want to say as well as you can say it. Above all, make sure that you have described your subject so vividly that your reader can "see" it.

How to Do It   Look at this example. Chandler used the revision checklist as he revised his draft. Here is a portion of his revised essay, showing some of the changes he made.

He added a descriptive word.

bustling
The ⌃crowd headed for the seats. Vendors were

selling programs. Eager fans, including us, were

trying to take it all in.

He added a phrase to make a sentence clearer.

over the crowd.
Stern police officers watched⌃The smell of hot

dogs, popcorn, and pizza made my mouth water.

There was the field, right in front of me! It was

He added a comparison to help his readers see what the grass was like.

bright green and perfectly clipped. It looked
like moss, not grass
~~smooth~~⌃. Players in fresh uniforms were throwing,

batting, and running.

That's when I thought I saw the ghosts. Babe

He replaced two vague phrases with strong images.

took a practice swing
Ruth⌃ ~~was there~~. Lou Gehrig waved to the crowd.
signed an autograph for a fan
Mickey Mantle⌃ ~~was there, too~~.

Apply It

▶ Use this revision checklist to guide you as you revise your work.

INTRODUCTION:

☐ Open with a sentence that will draw your readers into your description. If you did not, add a sentence now. If you did, make sure that it grabs the readers' attention.

☐ Give the readers an overall view of the subject. If you have not, add the sentences that you need now. If you have, try to make the impression stronger.

☐ Use vivid sensory details. If you have not, add some details now. If you have, try to use more specific nouns and adjectives.

☐ End with a sentence that leads your readers into the body of your essay. If you have not, add a sentence now.

BODY:

☐ Use vivid sensory details. If you have not, add some details now. If you have, try to use more specific nouns and adjectives.

☐ Present the details in a clear order. Use spatial order or order of importance. If details are out of order, rearrange them now.

☐ Group details in paragraphs. Group details about the same part of the subject. Group details by sense or by order of importance. If there are too many details in some paragraphs, divide the body into more paragraphs.

☐ Use transitional words and phrases to help the reader tell where details are. If transitions are missing, add them now.

CONCLUSION:

☐ Use vivid sensory details. If you have not, add some details now. If you have, try to use more specific nouns and adjectives.

☐ Return to the overall view of the subject. If you did not include a sentence that shows the whole picture, add one now.

☐ If you wish, tell the reader how you feel about the subject. If you did not do so, you may want to add a sentence now.

☐ End with an image that your reader will remember. If you did not do so, add a sentence now.

GENERAL:

☐ Use vivid words. Do not use bland words, such as *great*, *good*, or *nice*. Replace them with stronger, more specific words.

☐ Do not leave grammatical errors in your essay. Correct any that you find. You will take a closer look when you proofread.

▶ If you can, work with a partner to revise your work. Read each other's drafts. Use the revision checklist to find places that might be improved. Make helpful suggestions to improve each other's work.

▶ Think about your partner's suggestions for your essay. Make the final decisions yourself about what to change.

Lesson 2 Proofreading Your Essay

Proofreading is the process of finding and correcting errors in grammar, mechanics, and usage. Follow these steps for proofreading your essay.

What to Do

When you proofread, look for the little mistakes that you might have missed or ignored earlier.

When you are writing a draft, it is a good idea not to worry about grammar and spelling. When you are revising, you should focus on meaning rather than small mistakes. Now it is time to look for those mistakes. Read your work sentence by sentence and word by word. Use the proofreading checklist below to find and correct any mistakes.

How to Do It

Use the following checklist. It lists problems you may find in descriptive writing. You also will find a guide to grammar, mechanics, and usage on pages 76–80.

☐ Make subjects agree with their verbs in number. (Singular subjects need singular verbs. Plural subjects need plural verbs.)
☐ Use complete sentences. Correct any fragments. Correct any run-on sentences.
☐ Use pronouns correctly. Is it clear what noun each pronoun refers to?
☐ Use adjectives to modify nouns or pronouns. Use adverbs to modify verbs, adjectives, and other adverbs.
☐ End each sentence with a period, question mark, or exclamation point.
☐ Use apostrophes correctly in all contractions to show where letters have been taken out.
☐ Use apostrophes correctly to show possession.
☐ Punctuate dialogue correctly:
  ■ Use quotation marks to show where a person's exact words begin and end.
  ■ Use a comma after words that introduce a quotation: Chandler said, "The smell of pizza made my mouth water."
  ■ Use a comma after the quotation, inside the quotation marks, when an explanation follows a quotation: "The field looks like moss," Chandler said.
  ■ Place periods, question marks, and exclamation points inside quotation marks: Chandler said, "There's nothing like opening day at Yankee Stadium!"
  ■ Begin a new paragraph for each new speaker.
☐ Check the essay for spelling errors. If you are unsure about the spelling of certain words, use a dictionary.

Apply It

▶ Use the proofreading checklist to find errors in your work. Correct those errors now. If you can, work with a partner. A fresh eye may see errors that you missed.

Lesson 3 Publishing Your Essay

You have worked hard to prepare your essay and make it as good as you can make it. Now take it to your audience!

What to Do

Find the best way to reach your audience.

How will you publish your description? How can you be sure that your audience will see it or hear it? If you can, discuss ideas with a group of students. Consider everyone's suggestions, and then choose the plan that you feel is right.

How to Do It

Choose a way of publishing that suits your audience. Here are some suggestions.

Audience	Ways to Publish
Students or adults at school	Send your descriptive essay to the school literary magazine. Read your essay to your class. With your classmates, put together a collection of your essays to keep in the classroom.
Audiences outside school	Submit your descriptive essay to a magazine. Enter your descriptive essay in a writing contest. Post your descriptive essay on an on-line bulletin board. Duplicate copies for family and friends.

Review It

▶ A strong title will attract readers' attention and make them want to read the essay. Chandler thought of three possible titles for his essay:

"The Ghosts of Opening Day"
"What Opening Day at Yankee Stadium Is Like"
"My Trip to Yankee Stadium"

Underline the one that you like best.

Apply It

▶ Make a clean final copy of your narrative essay. Brainstorm a list of possible titles for your essay. Choose one. Then select one of the ways for publishing your essay.

What Have You Learned in Unit 2?

Use these questions to gather and review your thoughts about the importance of each of the key points in Unit 2. Don't worry about writing complete sentences. Just put some thoughts, ideas, and reactions down for each question.

1. Write one good topic for a three-to-five-paragraph descriptive essay.

_____

2. Why is it a good topic?

_____

3. What kinds of details do you need in a description?

_____

4. What should you put in the introduction to a descriptive essay?

_____

5. What should you put in the body of a descriptive essay?

_____

6. What should you put in the conclusion of a descriptive essay?

_____

7. What do you do when you revise?

_____

8. What do you do when you proofread?

_____

9. What did you enjoy most about writing your descriptive essay?

_____

10. What can you do next time to make the writing easier and more enjoyable?

_____

▶ If you can, share your answers with a partner or group. Share the ideas and experiences you had. Writing is always filled with unexpected twists and turns. Talk about what was funny or strange about your writing experience. Come up with a group list called "Tips for Writing Descriptive Essays."

UNIT 3 Writing on Your Own

There are many types of descriptive writing. You may already be familiar with essays that describe events, places, and objects. These different types of essays have the same purpose. They are written to show a reader what their subjects look, smell, taste, feel, or sound like.

What to Do

Become familiar with the three different kinds of descriptive essays that you will write in this unit.

A Description of an Event
A Travel Log
An Imaginary Description

How to Do It

Learn the key elements of each kind of essay that you will write.

A description of an event is like a motion picture. In an event, life is moving, and people are in action. To describe an event, you need words that capture the movement and action of life.

A travel log is a journal about a visit to another place. The place may be far away or around the corner. For a travel log, thinking about the audience is especially important. The writer's challenge is to describe the place for people who haven't been there. It may help to compare the new place with a place that is familiar to your audience.

As its name tells you, an imaginary description comes from your imagination. Creative writers let their imaginations run free. They create places that do not exist. An imaginary place may be the control room of a starship. It may be a hut that a shipwrecked sailor builds on an island. It may be a modern house that you would like to design. The details come from you. You build the place from your words.

Review It

▶ Find examples of each type of descriptive writing that you will write in this unit.

▶ Look for descriptions of events in magazines and newspapers. Look for travel writing in travel magazines and books. Look for descriptions of imaginary places in stories and novels. Save the examples in your notebook.

CHAPTER 1 Describing an Event

You have had a lot of practice describing events. You do it often when you talk with your family and friends. Anytime you start a sentence with words like "You should have been there . . ." you are about to describe an event. The purpose of a description of an event is to make your readers feel as if *they* were there.

What to Do
Learn what is unique about a description of an event. In a description of an event, you put your readers in the picture. Make them feel as if they are beside you as you experience the event.

How to Do It
Look at this example. It is the body and conclusion of a description that a student named Hank wrote for his school newspaper. The introduction is on page 7.

He described the event as if he and the readers were in it together.

He used action verbs that help readers picture the scene.

He used vivid adjectives.

He used specific words and phrases to name the objects in the scene.

He explained details that might not be familiar to some readers.

He ended by summing up his impressions of the event.

> The street vibrates to the beat of music. People clap hands and dance to a salsa band. Children laugh, shout, and tap their feet. The musicians' red satin shirts flutter in the spring breeze.
>
> Delicious smells drift from curbside carts. One vendor sells Middle-Eastern falafel. He fries chickpea patties until they are crisp. Then he serves them on bread with sesame sauce. Another vendor is making satay. It is a Thai dish. She dips strips of chicken into spicy peanut sauce. Then she grills them. A third vendor scoops cool mounds of Italian ice from a freezer. He displays them in a rainbow of colors.
>
> Everywhere people eat, talk, and laugh. They tug at one another's sleeves and point out the sights. They savor the wonderful food. They all agree that the fair is a feast. It is a feast for the eyes, the ears, and the taste buds.

Review It
1. Underline all the verbs in Hank's description.
2. List one detail that appeals to the sense of taste.

Lesson 1 Choosing a Topic

Have you ever attended a celebration or a festival? Have you ever attended a crowded sports event? These kinds of experiences make great topics for descriptions of events.

What to Do

Think about events that made strong impressions on you. These are likely to be the ones that are most meaningful to you. Those are the ones that you will describe best. Look for these qualities in an event to describe:

- Many people gathered in one place.
- Interesting action.
- Experiences for more than one sense.
- An emotional response.

Not every topic will have all of the qualities. One quality might stand out more than the others in some topics. For example, a football game might have exciting action. A graduation might have a very emotional response.

How to Do It

Use an idea branch to brainstorm topics.

Apply It

▶ Here's an idea branch of the kinds of events that make good topics for descriptions. Brainstorm ideas for each branch. Then choose the idea that appeals to you most.

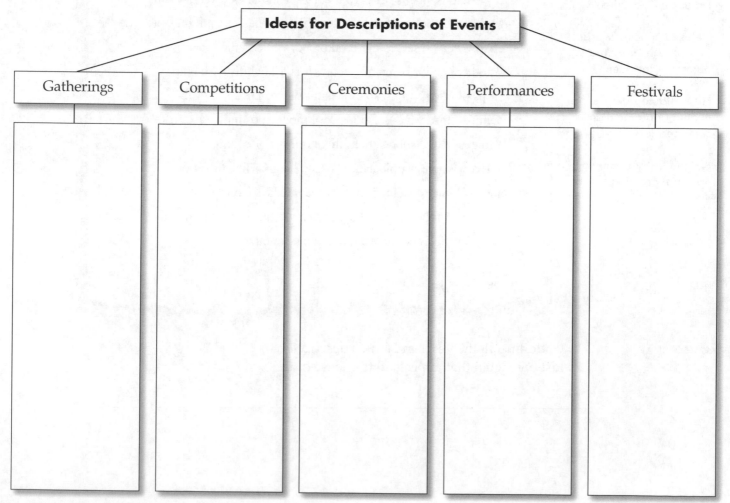

Ideas for Descriptions of Events

| Gatherings | Competitions | Ceremonies | Performances | Festivals |

Lesson 2 Gathering Details

Once you have chosen the topic of your description, gather details. For the introduction to your essay, you will need background details about the event. For the body, you will need details that appeal to the five senses.

What to Do

To gather background details, ask yourself *who, what, when, where, why*, and *how* questions. Then use a sensory details web to come up with vivid details.

How to Do It

Look at these examples. First, look at the questions and answers that Hank used to gather background details about the event. He planned to use these details in his introduction.

WHO was involved in the event?   me, people from Third Avenue, vendors,
                                                            musicians

WHAT was the event ?   the annual Third Avenue Street Fair
WHEN did the event take place?   one day in the spring
WHERE did the event take place?   all along Third Avenue
WHY did the event take place?   to bring people together, remind them
                                                    to be friendly

HOW did the event take place?   community organization, volunteers

Second, look at the web Hank created to gather sensory details. He planned to use these details in the body of his essay.

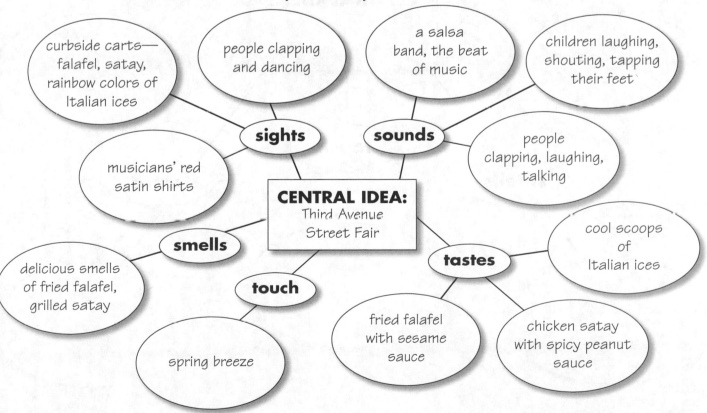

Apply It

▶ Gather the basic information and details you will need for your description of an event.

▶ First, ask yourself *who, what, when, where, why,* and *how* questions about your event. Write your answers on a separate sheet of paper. Keep these details for your introduction.

▶ Then use this sensory details web to gather vivid details. These details will bring the events in the body of your description to life. Add more ovals if you need them.

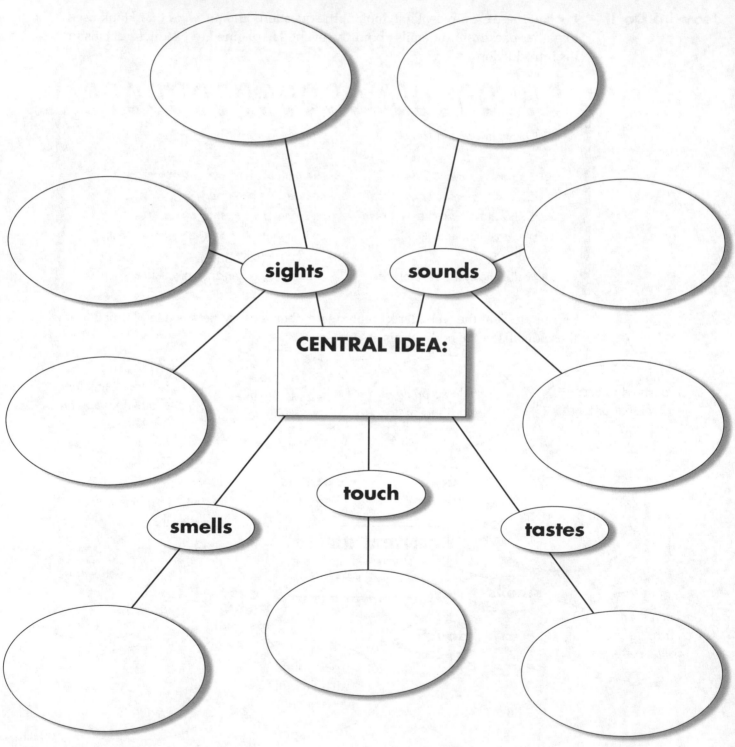

Lesson 3 Organizing Your Ideas

A description of an event contains an introduction, a body, and a conclusion.

What to Do Follow these hints to organize your description.

In the introduction, plan to give background information about the event. Use the answers to the *who, what, when, where, why,* and *how* questions you asked yourself on page 42. Finally, state your feelings about the event.

For the body, look at your sensory details web on page 42. Decide what details belong together. Plan to group details in paragraphs. Here are some ways that you can group them:

- Put details for the same sense, such as taste, together.
- Put details about similar subjects, such as food carts, together.
- Put details from the same location, such as near the musicians, together.

Plan the last sentence of your conclusion first. Make it a statement about your personal reactions to the event. Then jot notes for the rest of the sentences. These sentences will support the statement about your reactions. However, when you write the conclusion, you will put them before the reaction. They will lead the reader to it.

How to Do It Use a planning chart. Here is the one that Hank used.

INTRODUCTION
He gave background information about the event.
He stated his feelings.

> Usually, people pass one another without smiling or saying hello.
> Then the annual Third Avenue Street Fair arrives.
> People relax and slow down.
> The fair teaches people how to be friendly again!

BODY
He grouped related details.
He will include each group of details in a paragraph of its own.

> The street has the beat of music.
> The musicians have red satin shirts.
> People are clapping and dancing to a salsa band.
> Children are laughing, shouting, and tapping their feet.
>
> Curbside carts sell food.
> One vendor sells Middle-Eastern falafel.
> He serves it with sauce made from sesame seeds.
> Another vendor sells the Thai dish called satay.
> She cooks it with spicy peanut sauce.
> A third vendor scoops Italian ices from a freezer.

CONCLUSION
He wrote about his reactions to the event.
He wrote notes for the other sentences in the conclusion.

> LAST SENTENCE:
> The fair is a feast for the eyes, the ears, and the taste buds.
> All the people are eating, talking, and laughing.
> They point out the sights.
> They savor the wonderful food.

Apply It

▶ Use this planning chart to organize the details for your description. Jot some notes in the boxes. Make changes until you are satisfied with your plan.

INTRODUCTION
Give background information about the event. Use the answers to the *who, what, when, where, why,* and *how* questions you asked yourself on page 42. State your feelings about the event.

BODY
Group details from your sensory details web on page 42. Each group will become a paragraph.
Use one of these kinds of groups:
- Details for the same sense.
- Details about similar subjects.
- Details from the same locations.

CONCLUSION
Plan the last sentence first. Make it a statement about your personal reactions. Then jot notes for sentences that support your reactions.

Lesson 4 Writing Your Description of an Event

You have gathered details, taken notes, and organized your notes. Now you are ready to write your description.

What to Do Use your notes to write the draft of your description. Use the checklists on the next page to help you revise and proofread it.

How to Do It Look at this example. It is Hank's draft of the body of his essay. Notice how he used the revision and proofreading checklists to make improvements and fix mistakes. Take special note of the verbs he changed.

> **vibrates**
> The street ~~moves~~ to the beat of music.
> **clap hands and**
> People ^ dance to a salsa band. Children laugh,
> **tap**
> shout, and ~~move~~ their feet. The musicians' red
> **flutter**
> satin shirts ~~move~~ in the spring breeze.
>
> Delicious smells drift from curbside carts.
> **Middle-Eastern**
> One vendor sells ^ falafel. He fries chickpea
>
> patties until they are crisp. Then he serves
> **on bread**
> them ^ with sesame sauce. Another vendor is
> **strips of**
> making satay. It is a Thai dish. She dips ^
> **spicy**
> chicken into ^ peanut sauce. Then she grills
> **scoops**
> them. A third vendor ~~gets~~ cool mounds of
> **in a rainbow of colors**
> Italian ice from a freezer. He displays them ^.

Apply It

▶ On a separate sheet of paper, write your draft. Use the notes you made on pages 42 and 44. Do not worry about spelling and grammar right now. Focus on drafting a vivid description.

▶ After you have written the draft, read it. Then revise it. Use the checklist on page 34 and the one below, which focuses on key elements of a description of an event.

▶ When you have revised your draft, proofread it. Fix any mistakes in spelling, capitalization, punctuation, and grammar. Use the checklist on page 35 and the one below, which lists problems to be especially careful about in a description of an event.

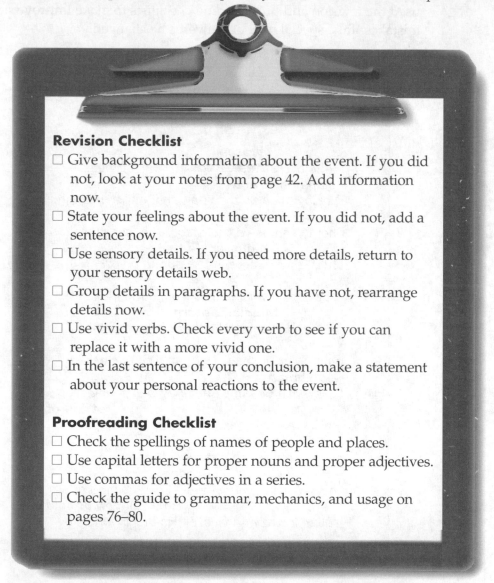

Revision Checklist
☐ Give background information about the event. If you did not, look at your notes from page 42. Add information now.
☐ State your feelings about the event. If you did not, add a sentence now.
☐ Use sensory details. If you need more details, return to your sensory details web.
☐ Group details in paragraphs. If you have not, rearrange details now.
☐ Use vivid verbs. Check every verb to see if you can replace it with a more vivid one.
☐ In the last sentence of your conclusion, make a statement about your personal reactions to the event.

Proofreading Checklist
☐ Check the spellings of names of people and places.
☐ Use capital letters for proper nouns and proper adjectives.
☐ Use commas for adjectives in a series.
☐ Check the guide to grammar, mechanics, and usage on pages 76–80.

▶ If you can, revise and proofread with a partner. Use the checklists to think of ways to improve your descriptions. Listen to your partner's suggestions.

▶ Once you have revised and proofread your description, make a clean copy of it. You may want to publish your description in one of the following ways:
  ■ Make it into a poster advertising the event.
  ■ Make it into a brochure promoting the event.
  ■ Submit it as an article for the school newspaper or a community newspaper.

CHAPTER 2 Writing a Travel Log

Travel gives us a new view of the world. We get new impressions from the places we visit. A travel log is a record of those impressions.

What to Do
Notice what is unique about a travel log. It captures your impressions from a trip. The details should be clear and strong. Your readers should feel as if they have traveled with you.

How to Do It
Here is part of a travel log that a student named Elise wrote. She was visiting New Orleans.

She dated her entries.

She reported her observations.

She used sensory details.

She included her reactions, opinions, and feelings.

She compared a new experience to one that is familiar to her audience

> June 3
>
> We got to our hotel in the French Quarter. This is the quaint, historic part of the city. Being here feels like going back in time. The streets are narrow. The antique buildings are like doll houses. Many of them have balconies with iron railings that look like vines.
>
> At dinner, my parents ordered oysters. New Orleans is famous for them. Oysters may be tasty, but they look gray and slimy. My father asked me to try one. All around me, people were eating them and smiling, but I just said, "N-o-o-o-o."
>
> After dinner, we listened to an exciting group of musicians playing jazz on the street. The banjo player's hands flew across the strings. He was really enjoying himself. He was wearing the same smile that the oyster-eaters wore.
>
> June 4
>
> In the morning we walked to the old market. At a lively cafe nearby we had beignets. They are puffy and almost round, like doughnuts without holes. They are dusted with powdered sugar and served warm. In my opinion, they are <u>much</u> better than oysters. After breakfast, we walked through the market. Vegetables and fish were laid out on in colorful displays. People were packing them in ice to keep them fresh.

Review It
1. Underline a sentence that shows how Elise felt about oysters.
2. Underline two sentences that describe beignets.

Apply It
▶ Plan a trip to write about. The trip may be around the block or around the world. If you are going to stay nearby, look at things as if you were a traveler from far away.

Lesson 1   Keeping a Travel Log

Vivid details are the key elements in a travel log, just as in any other description. Take vivid notes while you are traveling. You can use them to bring the final version to life for your readers.

What to Do

Do not try to write the finished version of your travel log while you are traveling. Do not even try to write the draft. Focus on observing. Jot down notes that will help you recall your observations. Keep in mind these three characteristics of a vivid detail:

- It is specific, not general.
- It appeals to at least one of the five senses.
- It is complete. No important piece of information is missing.

How to Do It

A great photographer, Walker Evans, once explained how to gather impressions. "Stare," he said. "It is the way to educate your eye, and more."

In addition to staring, take notes. Carry a small notebook. It should be small enough to fit in a pocket. As you travel, take time out to jot down your impressions in your notebook. Look at the following example. It is a page from the notebook that Elise carried in New Orleans.

She dated her entries.

She used just a phrase or a few words to help herself recall each impression.

Notice that she had not decided exactly what words to use in her description. She had not thought of *slimy* to describe the oysters when she wrote her notes.

June 3

French Quarter

old part of the city

narrow streets

old buildings with balconies

iron railings with twisty bars

quaint, where tourists come

looks the way it must have long ago

oysters at dinner

gray, wet, cold

everyone eating oysters—but not me!

musicians outside, on the street

old-time jazz

banjo player having a great time

Apply It

▶ Get ready for your trip by finding a small notebook. You can also fold sheets of plain paper so that they fit in your pocket.

▶ Take your trip. As you travel, look closely. Stare. From time to time, stop to take notes. Remember that you do not have to write sentences. You do not even have to find exactly the right words. You will find the right words and build sentences from your notes later on.

Lesson 2 Using Connotations

Every word has a specific meaning. A word might also have a suggested meaning, or tone. The tone of the word might be positive or negative. The tone of a word is called its connotation.

What to Do

Use words that show your feelings about the details you include. Choose your words carefully. Use words that have positive connotations for details that you enjoyed. Use words with negative connotations for details that you did not enjoy.

For example, the word *old* has a specific meaning. It means "not new." The words *antique* and *old-fashioned* have meanings similar to the meaning of *old*. They have different connotations. Note the positive and negative connotations of the following words:

NEUTRAL	POSITIVE	NEGATIVE
old buildings	antique buildings	old-fashioned buildings
narrow streets	snug streets	cramped streets
wet oysters	moist oysters	slimy oysters
busy cafe	lively cafe	noisy cafe

How to Do It

Elise used this diagram to come up with words with the connotations she wanted.

First, she listed details she wanted to include in her travel log. Then she jotted down descriptive words and phrases about each detail. She wrote down every word and phrase that came to mind. Then she checked the ones that had the connotations she wanted. Here is part of her diagram.

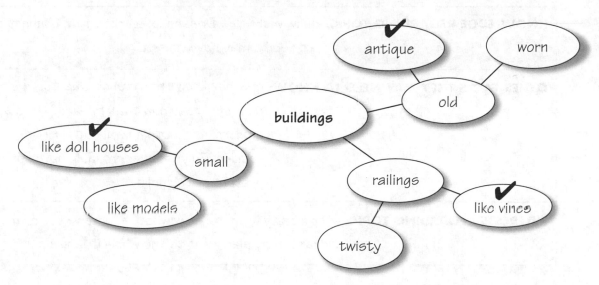

Apply It

▶ On a separate sheet of paper, create your own diagram for the details you have observed. For each detail, jot down descriptive words and phrases. Check the words and phrases that have the connotations you want.

Lesson 3 Identifying the Audience

Describe the place you visit so that *all* your readers can experience it. Explain the details so that every reader will understand them.

What to Do

Before you write, think about who your readers are. Assume that your audience has not been to the place you are describing. Decide the following things about your audience:

- their ages and experience
  (Are they classmates or are they younger students? Are they adults, such as the school principal or a teacher?)
- what they already know about the place
- what they might need to know to understand your description fully
  (What background descriptions should you provide?)
- what they may especially want to know about the place

How to Do It

Make an audience profile.

Before Elise began to write her travel log, she took some time to think about her audience. She made a profile for them. This is the profile she made:

TOPIC: my visit to French Quarter of New Orleans
AUDIENCE: my classmates and teacher
AGE RANGE/POSITION: adult; principal of school
KNOWLEDGE REGARDING TOPIC: know where New Orleans is; think of it in connection to jazz; some may have visited
OTHER FACTS THEY MAY NEED TO KNOW: may not know that French Quarter is old part of city; may not know that most of the city is modern; may not know about New Orleans cooking, Cajun foods; probably have not eaten oysters or beignets
INTERESTS REGARDING TOPIC: will probably want to know what is "different" about New Orleans; may also want to know how it is like our city

Apply It

▶ Think of possible audiences for your travel log. Choose one. On a separate sheet of paper, complete an audience profile.

Lesson 4 Writing Your Travel Log

Now you are ready to write the draft of your travel log. In the drafting stage, the point is to get your words on paper. Focus on what you want to say. You can improve the way you say it later.

What to Do

Write your descriptions as entries in a log, or journal. After you have written the draft, read it. Then revise it. When you have revised your draft, proofread it. Fix any mistakes in spelling, capitalization, punctuation, and grammar.

The best way to write the draft is to begin at the start of your trip and work right through to the end. If you find yourself struggling with one part, skip ahead. You can go back to the other part later. Follow this checklist to write your draft:

- ☐ Look back over your notes to refresh your memory.
- ☐ Think about what the whole experience meant to you. Keep that in mind as you write.
- ☐ Look over your audience profile. Keep your audience in mind as you write.
- ☐ Use your notes as the outline for your draft.

How to Do It

Use the revision checklist on page 34 and the one below, which focuses on key elements of a travel log.

- ☐ Be sure that you use vivid details to bring the place to life for your readers. If you don't think your details are vivid enough, improve them now.
- ☐ Show your feelings about the place you visited. If you have not, add sentences now.
- ☐ Use words with connotations that match your feelings. Do not use too many neutral words. Those are words that show no feeling. Replace them with words with strong connotations.
- ☐ Use transitional words to show where details are located. If you have not, add them now.

Apply It

Use the proofreading checklist on page 35 as you proofread your travel log.

▶ On a separate sheet of paper, draft your travel log. Use the notes that you have made. Do not worry about spelling and grammar right now. Get your ideas down on paper.

▶ If you can, revise and proofread with a partner. Suggest ways to improve each other's work and correct errors. Finally, when you are satisfied that your travel log is the best it can be, make a clean copy. Choose one of the following options for publishing your travel log.
- ■ Read your log aloud to a small group of classmates.
- ■ Give your log to a friend or relative who is interested in the place you visited.
- ■ Put together a class collection of travel logs. Use the style of a travel magazine.

CHAPTER 3 Writing an Imaginary Description

Where would you like to go? Would you like to travel to an outpost on a distant planet? Would you like to go to a tropical island? Would you like to visit a city of the future? You can go to any of these places—in your imagination.

What to Do

Learn the key elements of an imaginary description:
- It creates a vivid picture of an imaginary place.
- It uses details from your imagination.
- It is written for readers who know nothing about the place, except what you tell them.
- It reveals how you feel about the place.

How to Do It

Look at this example. It is an imaginary description that a student named Samir wrote. Samir wrote his description with three parts—an introduction, a body, and a conclusion.

A shark peers in through the window. Behind the shark, dozens of yellow puffer fish swim past. Beyond them, the sea is dark. This is my view from the cafeteria. The time is some day in the future. I live in a colony far beneath the sea. It does not feel much like home.

The smooth metal walls sometimes seem cold. The plain cafeteria food does not taste much like home, either. All of us bring spicy sauces back from trips "up above." We add them to our dinners.

Down here, we never see daylight. Floodlights make the water glow nearby. Beyond that it is always night. Strange fish swim out of the night and into the light. Some have huge eyes, and others have no eyes at all.

At night, I get into my bunk. I inhale the odorless filtered air. The purring of the air pumps makes me drowsy. I fall asleep remembering the sound of city traffic.

Apply It

▶ Imagine a place to write about. It may help you to look through magazines and clip pictures of places. Imagine yourself in the place you choose. What do you want to tell people about it? In your notebook, jot down ideas.

Lesson 1 Imagining Details

When you write about a place that does not exist, you have to make up the details.

What to Do
Use the usual ways of gathering sensory details. However, you will not be remembering or noticing details. You will be making them up. Keep these hints in mind as you gather details:

- Imagine yourself in the place. Try one of these tricks to help you:
  - Look at pictures that suggest your place.
  - Create pictures that suggest your place.
  - Play music or other sounds that suggest your place.
- Look around you with your "mind's eye." Take notes on what you see.
- Touch the things around you. Take notes on what you feel.
- Listen to the sounds around you. Take notes on what you hear.
- Sniff the air around you. Take notes on what you smell.
- Sample the foods around you. Take notes on what you taste.

How to Do It
Samir made a sensory details web to help himself imagine details. Before he began, he spread pictures of unusual sea creatures in front of him. Then he made a sketch of the underwater colony. Finally, he followed the hints above and took notes.

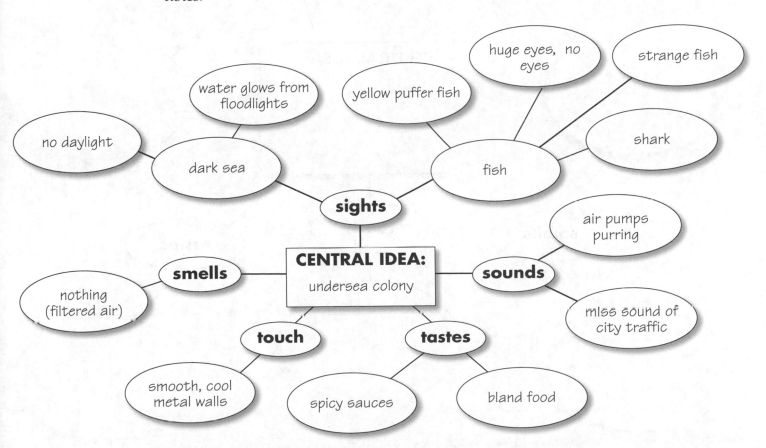

▶ Imagine the details you will need for your description. Use this sensory details web to gather the vivid details that will bring your imaginary place to life.

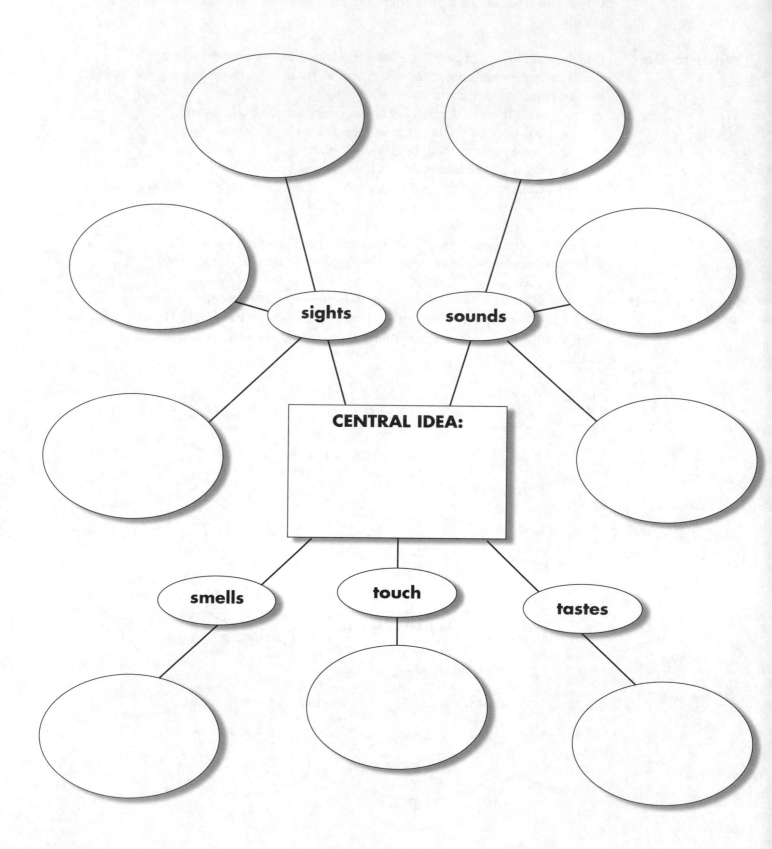

Lesson 2 Organizing Imaginary Details

Sensory details will help your readers experience your imaginary place. However the details must be in a clear order. Organization is especially important when you are describing a place your readers have never seen.

What to Do

You can organize your imaginary description in many different ways. Here are three ways:

- A Guided Tour
  Take your readers on a tour of the place. Imagine the readers arriving there. Walk the readers through the place from the entrance to the exit. Spatial organization will work best.
- A Frozen Moment
  Imagine that you have taken a photograph of the place. It is frozen in the picture. Describe what the picture shows. Spatial organization will work best.
- An Overall Impression
  Decide how the place makes you feel. Think about what its "atmosphere" is like. Use details to show why you feel as you do. Order of importance is the best organization.

How to Do It

Samir used the "Overall Impression" organization for the essay that you saw on page 52. He also thought about using the "Guided Tour" method of organization. Look at his notes for that:

A Guided Tour of the Underwater Colony
- Enter the "bubble taxi," a glass ball, shiny
- Travel down to the colony, see colorful fish
- Into dark waters, no sounds but equipment
- Enter colony, clang of door, echoes in corridor
- Gleaming metal everywhere, high-tech gear hums
- Observation center, video screens on every desk
- Video shows creatures on screens
- Screens show strange fish with huge eyes
- Move on to cafeteria, windows show glowing sea
- Visit my room, tiny, with pictures of home on walls
- Walk along long corridor, glass above and below
- Leave through door to taxi, clang of door closing

Review It

▶ Underline the words and phrases that name specific places in the underwater colony.

Apply It

▶ Choose a method of organization for your imaginary description. On a separate sheet of paper, organize your notes to match the method you choose.

Lesson 3 Writing Your Imaginary Description

Now you are ready to write the first draft of your own imaginary description.

What to Do Use your notes to write the draft of your imaginary description. After you have written the draft, read it. Then revise it. When you have revised your draft, proofread it. Fix any mistakes in spelling, capitalization, punctuation, and grammar.

How to Do It Use the hints in the following chart. First, find the method of organization you chose. Then follow the steps to write your draft.

	GUIDED TOUR	FROZEN MOMENT	OVERALL IMPRESSION
INTRODUCTION	■ Grab the readers' attention with a sentence welcoming the readers to the place. ■ Show the readers a part of the place that will make a strong first impression.	■ Grab the readers' attention with a "wide-angle" view. ■ "Zoom in" on the one outstanding detail that you think is most important or most interesting.	■ Grab the readers' attention with a description of one outstanding detail (like a shark outside the window). ■ Express your feelings about the place.
BODY	■ Write a paragraph that walks the readers through the place and stops at a special part of it. ■ Write a second paragraph about the special part.	■ Write a paragraph about the less-important details around the outstanding one. ■ Write a second paragraph about the outstanding detail.	■ Write a paragraph that describes a feature that supports your feelings. ■ Write a second paragraph that describes another feature that supports your feelings.
CONCLUSION	■ Bring your reader to the exit. ■ Remind the readers of the first impression.	■ Pull back to the overall picture. ■ Finish with a last sentence about the outstanding detail.	■ Return to your feelings. ■ Leave your readers with an image they will remember.

To revise your draft, use the checklist on page 34 and the one below, which focuses on key elements of an imaginary description. To help you proofread, use the checklist on page 35 and the one below, which focuses on problems in an imaginary description.

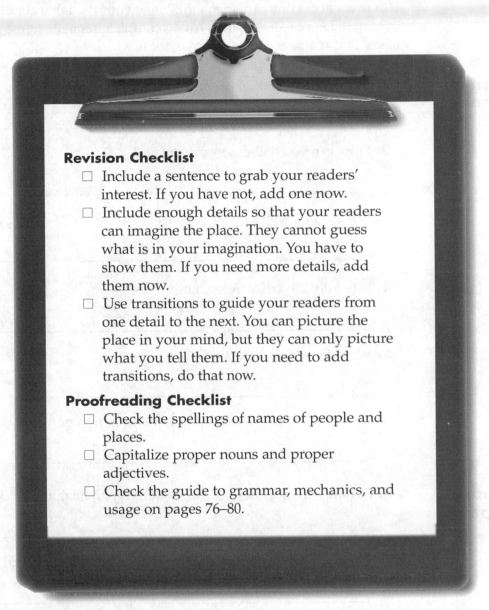

Revision Checklist
☐ Include a sentence to grab your readers' interest. If you have not, add one now.

☐ Include enough details so that your readers can imagine the place. They cannot guess what is in your imagination. You have to show them. If you need more details, add them now.

☐ Use transitions to guide your readers from one detail to the next. You can picture the place in your mind, but they can only picture what you tell them. If you need to add transitions, do that now.

Proofreading Checklist
☐ Check the spellings of names of people and places.

☐ Capitalize proper nouns and proper adjectives.

☐ Check the guide to grammar, mechanics, and usage on pages 76–80.

Apply It

▶ On a separate sheet of paper, write your draft.

▶ Use the checklists above to revise your draft.

▶ If you can, exchange descriptions with a partner. Proofread each other's descriptions for spelling, grammar, and punctuation errors.

▶ After you have written, revised, and proofread your description, make a clean copy. You may want to add illustrations.

▶ As a class, collect the imaginary descriptions in a folder or binder. You may want to make a cover for the collection. Brainstorm a title, such as "Voyages to Imaginary Places."

What Have You Learned in Unit 3?

Use these questions to gather and review your thoughts about the writing you did in Unit 3. Don't worry about writing complete sentences. Just put some thoughts, ideas, and reactions down for each question.

Description of an Event

1. How can you gather background details for a description of an event?

   _____

2. How can you gather sensory details?

   _____

3. What is one way to group details in the body of a description of an event?

   _____

Travel Log

4. What do you tell about in a travel log?

   _____

5. What makes a detail vivid?

   _____

6. Why is it important to keep your readers in mind when writing a travel log?

   _____

Imaginary Description

7. What is one way of gathering details for an imaginary description?

   _____

8. What is one way of organizing an imaginary description?

   _____

9. Which method of organization did you use for your imaginary description? Why?

   _____

10. Why is it especially important to include many details in an imaginary description?

    _____

▶ If you can, share your answers with a partner or group. Talk about the ideas and experiences you had. Share problems and successes you had while writing. Develop a group list of tips for each kind of writing you did in this unit.

UNIT 4 Writing on Assignment

Sometimes, you will be told what to write. You will be given an assignment. This is true of adult writers, too. In all types of careers, people have writing to do as part of their jobs. Often, their writing assignments have deadlines. A deadline is the time when a writing project must be completed. To meet a deadline, you may have to shorten some of the writing steps.

What to Do   Become familiar with the two different kinds of description that you will write in this unit:

A Test Essay
A Technical Description

How to Do It   Learn the key elements of each kind that you will write.

A test essay is unique in two important ways.

First, it is written in response to a question or a set of directions. You have to make sure that you answer the question or follow the directions.

Second, a test essay is written under a deadline. You must work quickly and efficiently. You must organize your thoughts as quickly as possible. You must limit your answer to what you can write before the deadline. You will not have much time to revise. You will be able to make only the most important changes.

A technical description shows a reader the parts of an object. It may describe the parts of a battery, the human heart, or a stereo system. It shows how the parts are related and how they fit together. It uses words with special meanings, called technical terms.

Apply It   ▶ Find examples of each type of description you will write in this unit. Look for an essay you have written for a test. Look for technical descriptions in encyclopedias and in owners' manuals. If you can, work with a group to discuss how the writers of the examples (including you) have written their descriptions. Save the examples in your notebook.

CHAPTER 1 Writing a Test Essay

Many tests in English and social studies classes include essays. Often, a test will ask you to read a statement and then describe something in a short essay. Your teacher will expect you to include sensory details and arrange them in order. You can do well on essay tests by understanding the test questions and organizing your answers.

What to Do

Learn what is unique about a test essay. A test essay is a short piece of writing that tells what you know about a topic. This type of essay follows the standard format of all descriptive essays. It has an introduction, body, and conclusion. However, a test essay is unique. Most often, it is written in response to a prompt. A prompt is a question or a set of directions. Here is a sample test prompt.

> Jack Finney's short story "The Third Level" begins in New York City in the present time. A man named Charley takes a wrong turn in Grand Central Station and finds himself in Galesburg, Illinois, in 1894. Use sensory details to describe Galesburg. Describe Charley's reactions to it. Give details from the story that describe how life in 1894 was different from life today.

How to Do It

Study this example. It is the beginning of an essay that a student named Josh wrote for an English test.

> When Charley arrives in Galesburg, Illinois, in 1894, he thinks he has found paradise. Charley decides that he would like to live there—if it is real.
>
> For Charley, Galesburg is an escape from hectic modern life. It is peaceful and calm. We can see this from the way he describes the place. He says that in 1894 "summer evenings were twice as long." He means that life was much more relaxed.
>
> The people of Galesburg do not rush to movies and restaurants and malls as people do now. They sit out on their lawns just enjoying the natural beauty around them.

Review It

1. List three words or phrases that Josh used to describe Charley's reactions to Galesburg.

_____

_____

_____

2. Look at the second paragraph. A phrase there shows that Josh is describing Charley's reactions. What phrase is it?

_____

3. Look at the third paragraph. A phrase there shows that Josh is describing how life in 1894 was different from life today. What phrase is it?

_____

▶ Read the rest of Josh's test essay. Then follow the directions below it.

> Evenings are quiet in Galesburg, because television and radio do not exist. There are no noisy cars or roaring planes in 1894. There are no humming air conditioners. People talk quietly while fireflies flicker soundlessly around them.
>
> Galesburg in 1894 is such a peaceful world that Charley wants to go back there. He wants to live there, in the past, not in the present.

4. What is one detail that appeals to the sense of hearing?

_____

5. What is one detail that appeals to the sense of sight?

_____

6. According to Josh, what is Charley's overall reaction to Galesburg?

_____

Lesson 1 Understanding the Prompt

Most test essays have to be planned and written quickly. You have only a certain amount of time before the test period is over. Therefore, you must organize your thoughts as quickly as possible.

What to Do

The key to writing a great test essay is to focus on the prompt and do what it says. Follow these two important steps:

- Read the prompt at least twice.
- Decide exactly what it asks you to do or tells you to do.

The questions or directions in the prompt will become your reasons for writing.

How to Do It

Study the prompt from Josh's essay test as an example. Note the key words that Josh underlined.

> Jack Finney's short story "The Third Level" begins in New York City in the present time. A man named Charley takes a wrong turn in Grand Central Station and finds himself in Galesburg, Illinois, in 1894. Use sensory details to describe Galesburg. Describe Charley's reactions to it. Give details from the story that describe how life in 1894 was different from life today.

Josh analyzed the prompt to understand the assignment. He found the key words *use*, *sensory details*, *describe*, and *give*. These words showed him that he had to do three things:

1. Describe Galesburg, using sensory details.
2. Describe Charley's reactions to Galesburg.
3. Describe how life in 1894 was different from life today, using details from the story.

Apply It

▶ Read this prompt. Underline key words and phrases that tell what the purpose for writing is.

> Gwendolyn Brooks's short story "Home" is about people who fear that they may lose their house. To keep themselves from feeling miserable, they try not to like the house. Describe the house, and describe the neighborhood around it. Include details that show how the family pretends to feel about it.

Lesson 2 Organizing Your Thoughts Quickly

When you answer a test prompt, you must **limit** your answer to what you can cover in a few paragraphs. You do not have much time, so you have to get organized quickly.

What to Do   Use the prompt to help you organize your answer. Use your list of the key steps in answering the prompt as your outline. If you have trouble remembering sensory details, make a details web.

How to Do It   Study this example. These are the notes that Josh made. Notice that in his details web he left some blanks. There were no sensory details for touch and taste in "The Third Level."

1. people sitting out on their lawns
   natural beauty
   quiet evenings
   fireflies
2. seems like paradise, would like to live there,
   may not be real, peaceful and calm, an escape
   from hectic life, wants to go back
3. life is much more relaxed
   -"summer evenings were twice as long"
   -people do not rush
   -no movies, malls, television, radio, cars, planes,
    air conditioners (just fans)

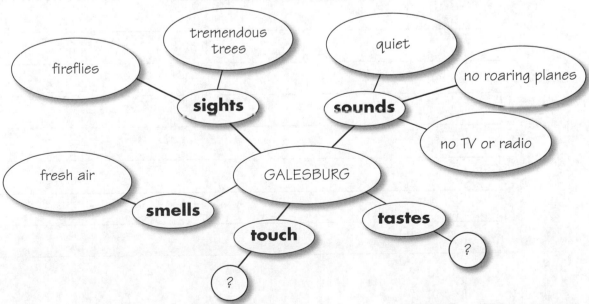

Apply It

▶ Look back at the test prompt that you analyzed on page 62. Find Gwendolyn Brooks's short story "Home" and read it so that you can answer the prompt. If you cannot find the story, use the following as a test prompt.

> Suppose that Charley from Jack Finney's short story "The Third Level" traveled to your neighborhood instead of Galesburg, Illinois. Describe your neighborhood, and describe what Charley's reactions to it would be. Include details that describe how life in your neighborhood is different from life in Galesburg.

▶ On the lines below, quickly jot down notes to organize ideas for your answer. Give yourself a time limit of 5 to 10 minutes.

_____

_____

_____

_____

_____

_____

_____

_____

_____

_____

_____

_____

_____

Lesson 3 Drafting Under a Deadline

A deadline is a writer's term for the date or time when a writing project must be completed. To meet a deadline, you may have to shorten some of the writing steps.

What to Do

Adjust to the deadline. You may have only thirty minutes to an hour to complete your essay. Therefore, you must work as quickly and efficiently as possible.

How to Do It

These tips will help you to get organized and draft your descriptive test essay.

Organizing

- Quickly jot down notes. Use your analysis of the prompt as your outline. Look your notes over. Make sure that they are clear and complete.
- Make a details web to help yourself recall details for each sense.

Drafting

- Do not let the time pressure get to you. Relax. You have analyzed the prompt and made complete notes. The most difficult part of the assignment is over.
- Write or print as neatly as possible. Because this is a test, you probably will not be able to make a fresh final copy of your essay.
- Skip a line between lines of writing. These blank lines will leave you space to make revisions and proofreading corrections later.
- Follow these steps to complete your draft quickly. Refer to your outline as you write.

  - Introduction
    Begin with a sentence that tells what description will follow.
    Meet any requirements of the prompt that may not come up in the rest of the essay. For example: "Tell where the story takes place."

  - Body
    Write a paragraph for each section of your outline.

  - Conclusion
    End with a sentence that sums up what your reader has just read.

Apply It

▶ On a separate sheet of paper, write a complete draft of your test essay. Use the notes you made on page 64. If you wish, set a time limit for yourself so that you can practice writing under a deadline. Allow yourself 30 minutes in total to respond to the prompt. Spend 5 to 10 minutes planning and organizing. Spend about 15 minutes writing the draft. That should leave you 5 to 10 minutes to revise and proofread in Lesson 4.

Lesson 4 Completing a Test Essay

When you are working under a deadline, you will not have time to make all the changes you would like to make. Make the ones that affect the meaning of your work first. Those are the most important ones.

What to Do   Finish the draft of your essay before your time is up. You want to have enough time in the test period to go over it quickly.

How to Do It   Because you are taking a test, you will not be able to revise and proofread with a partner. Make any changes that you feel will improve your test essay. Write or print as neatly as possible. Make it clear where words and phrases should be inserted. Rely on your own good judgment, and use these checklists for help.

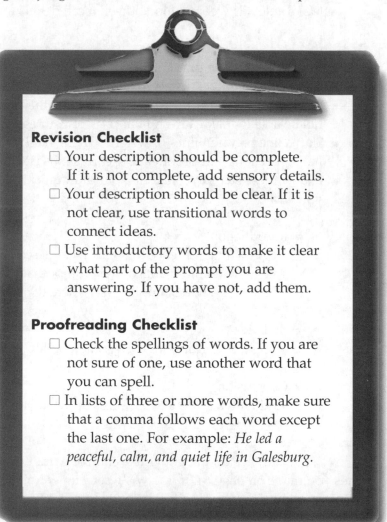

Revision Checklist
- ☐ Your description should be complete. If it is not complete, add sensory details.
- ☐ Your description should be clear. If it is not clear, use transitional words to connect ideas.
- ☐ Use introductory words to make it clear what part of the prompt you are answering. If you have not, add them.

Proofreading Checklist
- ☐ Check the spellings of words. If you are not sure of one, use another word that you can spell.
- ☐ In lists of three or more words, make sure that a comma follows each word except the last one. For example: *He led a peaceful, calm, and quiet life in Galesburg.*

Apply It   ▶ Revise and proofread the draft of your test essay. Work right on the draft. Make the changes as neatly as you can.

▶ If you can, meet with a small group of students when you have finished. Share your test essays. Discuss the process of writing a test essay. Which parts were difficult? Which parts seemed easier? Help each other to relax regarding test essays. They will become easier to write now that you have built your descriptive writing skills!

CHAPTER 2 Writing a Technical Description

A technical description helps readers understand an object. It points out the parts of the object. It shows how they fit together and work together.

Writing technical descriptions is a great career for someone who has skills in descriptive writing. People need to understand the objects around them. Those objects range from stereo sets to the human heart.

What to Do
Learn the key elements of a technical description.
- Visual aids that increase the audience's understanding
- Headings to break information into smaller parts
- Descriptive details about the object
- Details that increase the audience's understanding
- Specific words to name specific parts (technical terms)
- Explanations of terms that the audience might not know

How to Do It
Study this portion of a technical description of a CD player. It was written by a group of students. Note the key elements.

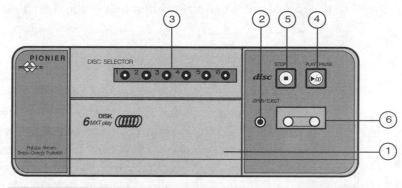

A drawing helps readers see where parts are located.

An introduction gives an overall description of the object.

Headings break the description into parts.

Descriptive details about each part are included.

All the controls are on the front of the CD player. There are three main types of controls. They work the disc tray, the disc selector, and playback. Each type is described in detail below.

Disc Tray Controls

The disc tray (1) holds the compact discs to be played. It is in the center of the player, at the bottom. The open/close button (2) is to the right of the tray. It opens and closes the tray.

Disc Selector Controls

The disc selector buttons (3) are located along the top of the player. They allow you to choose which disc to play. The tray holds up to six discs. Each button is numbered to show which disc it controls.

Review It

1. What type of object is described?

_____

2. What are the three main parts?

_____

_____

_____

3. What is one technical term that the writers used?

_____

4. What explanation did they give for that term?

_____

_____

▶ Read the rest of the description. Then follow the directions below it.

Playback Controls

    Four buttons control the playback of a disc. The play button (4) is on the far right of the player. It starts the playback. The stop button (5) is to the left of the play button. It stops playback. The two search buttons (6) are below the play and stop buttons. They let you go from one song to another on a disc. The forward search button is on the right. The backward search button is on the left.

    The controls for the disc tray, disc selector, and playback are all on the front of the player. You do not need to touch the back of the player. With the push of a button, the CD player is under your control.

5. Underline words and phrases that tell where parts are located.

Apply It

▶ For this project, you might work alone, with a partner, or with a small group. Begin by finding examples of technical descriptions. Flip through owners' manuals, instruction booklets and science books. Copy good examples in your notebook.

▶ Then think of an object you might describe. It could be a household appliance, such as a VCR or blender. It could be something in science, such as a blood cell. Brainstorm for ten minutes, jotting down every idea that comes to you. Then choose one object as the topic for your technical description.

Lesson 1   Helping the Audience

In this project, you are a technical writer. Your job is to help your audience understand what you describe. First, identify who the readers are likely to be. Then write to make the object clear to this audience.

What to Do

Think about the people who need to know about the object you chose. Do not tell them more than they need to know. Do not tell them less than they need to know. Think about these questions:

- What are the most important parts of the object?
- Which parts are easiest to understand?
- Which parts are hardest to understand?
- What audience will be most interested in this object? Think about their age and knowledge.
- Why will the audience want to know about the object?

How to Do It

List details to suit your audience. These will become the details that you use in your description.

Use an audience needs chart to list details that will match the needs of the audience. Here is an audience needs chart for the CD player.

Topic: CD player	
Audience: new users of the CD player	
Audience Needs to Know	**Details to Match Audience Needs**
where CDs go	disc tray open/close button
what controls play CDs	play button stop button

what controls choose tracks on a CD	search buttons
	   forward
	   backward

what controls change CDs	disc selector buttons

Apply It

▶ Make your own audience needs chart. Start the chart by using the answers to the questions in What to Do. Add any new ideas that come to you. Think about the details of your object that will match the needs of your audience.

Lesson 2 Organizing Information

You have decided what information you need to give your audience. Now it is time to decide how to present that information.

What to Do

Follow these hints:

- Your introduction can be as short as three sentences. First, identify the object. Then present the major parts. Describe them briefly if it seems necessary. Finally, write a sentence that leads into the details that follow.
- To plan the body of your essay, look at your audience needs chart. Write a heading for each feature that the audience needs to know. List details under each heading.
- Plan to keep your conclusion to two or three sentences. Summarize the major parts again. Add any extra information your audience may need. End with an overall description or a positive statement.

How to Do It

Use a planning chart. Here is the one that the writers used to organize the description of the CD player.

INTRODUCTION
They identified the object.
They presented the major parts.
They led the reader into the details that follow.

> All controls are on the front of the CD player.
> There are three main types of controls.
> They work the disc tray, the disc selector, and playback.
> Each type is described in detail below.

BODY
They created headings from the notes on the audience needs chart.

They listed details under each heading.

> Disc Tray Controls
> Disc tray in the center of the player, at the bottom.
> Open/close button to the right of the tray.
>
> Disc Selector Controls
> Disc selector buttons along the top of the player.
> Numbered to show which discs they control.
>
> Playback Controls
> Play button on the far right of the player.
> Stop button to the left of the play button.
> Search buttons below the play and stop buttons.

CONCLUSION
They summarized the major parts again.
They added useful information.
They finished with a positive statement.

> Controls for the disc tray, disc selector, and playback are all on the front of the player.
> You do not need to touch the back of the player.
> The CD player is under your control.

Apply It

▶ Complete your own planning chart. Use the chart to organize your thoughts on your object. Jot some notes in the boxes. Make changes until you are satisfied with your plan.

Lesson 3 Using Technical Terms

Every object has a name, of course. The parts of objects have names, too. Some of these names are familiar to almost everybody. Some of them are not. They are special words with special uses. These are technical terms.

What to Do
Use and explain technical terms. There may be technical terms for parts of the object you describe. Since they are the best names for the parts, they are the words you should use. However, your audience may not know the terms. Keep your audience in mind. You may have to explain these terms in your description.

For example, the word *eject* can have a special meaning. It can mean "take a compact disc out of a CD player." Here are some other technical terms that have to do with stereo equipment.

TECHNICAL TERM	EXPLANATION OR DEFINITION
magazine	box that holds a few CDs at once
tone	how high or low the music sounds
volume	how loud the sound is
band	AM or FM radio signals

How to Do It
List the technical terms that you plan to use. Think of an explanation for each one.

The writers of the CD player description used this chart to come up with explanations for technical terms.

Technical Term	Explanation or Definition
disc tray	holds the compact discs to be played
open/close button	opens and closes the tray
disc selector buttons	allow you to choose which disc to play
play button	starts the playback
stop button	stops playback
search buttons	let you go from one song to another on a disc

Apply It
▶ On a separate sheet of paper, create your own chart for the technical terms that you plan to use.

▶ For each detail of your product, jot down descriptive words and phrases. Check the words and phrases that are technical terms. Write explanations that will make the terms clear to your audience.

Lesson 4 Drafting Your Technical Description

Now you are ready to write a draft of your description. You will also need to sketch a picture or diagram of your object.

What to Do

First, sketch your object. Label the important parts. If you do not have room for the names of the parts, number them. You can refer to the numbers in your description.

Then draft your description. Be sure that it matches the drawing or diagram.

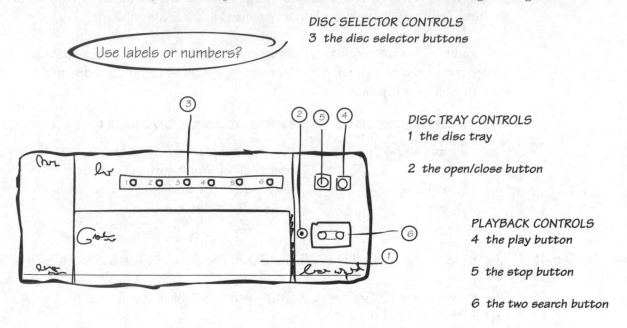

DISC SELECTOR CONTROLS
3 the disc selector buttons

Use labels or numbers?

DISC TRAY CONTROLS
1 the disc tray

2 the open/close button

PLAYBACK CONTROLS
4 the play button

5 the stop button

6 the two search button

How to Do It

When drafting your description, you may want to use the following checklist:

- ☐ Identify the object.
- ☐ Present the major parts. Describe them briefly if it seems necessary.
- ☐ Write a sentence that leads into the details that follow.
- ☐ Look at the chart you made on page 69. Write a heading for each feature that the audience needs to know.
- ☐ Describe details under each heading.
- ☐ Use words and phrases to tell where the parts of the object are.
- ☐ Explain technical terms that your audience may not know.
- ☐ Summarize the major parts in the conclusion.
- ☐ Add any extra information your audience may need.
- ☐ End with an overall description or a positive statement.

Apply It

▶ Sketch your drawing or diagram. Do not worry about the roughness of your sketch right now. Later, you will make the final copy.

▶ Write your draft. Use your notes from Lessons 1, 2, and 3. Be sure to keep your audience in mind.

Lesson 5 Completing Your Technical Description

Finish your technical description by revising the text and the art. When it is ready for the public, put it to the test. See whether people can understand the parts of the object you described.

What to Do

If you are working with a group, use everyone's skills and talents. Have the best writers revise and proofread the copy. Have the best artists revise and polish the art. Have the whole group brainstorm ways to publish the completed work.

If you are working alone, try to "step back" from your work and look at it with a fresh eye.

How to Do It

Use the revision checklist on page 34. Use the proofreading checklist on page 35. Also use the checklists below, which focus on key elements and proofreading problems in a technical description.

Revision Checklist

- ☐ The introduction should identify the object and present the major parts. If it does not, correct it now.
- ☐ Headings should divide the body into parts that are easy to read. Add headings if you need them.
- ☐ Descriptive words and phrases should show the readers where the parts of the object are. Add any that are needed.
- ☐ Explain technical terms that the audience may not know. If you did not, do it now.

Proofreading Checklist

- ☐ Check the spellings of technical terms.
- ☐ Check the guide to grammar, mechanics, and usage on pages 76–80.

Apply It

▶ Test your description before you revise and proofread it. Have a sample audience read the description and look at your diagram. If the sample audience cannot follow your description, revise it to make it clearer.

▶ If you can, meet with a small group of classmates. Have the group members be your sample audience. Share ideas and suggestions with each other to make your descriptions even better. Make any changes that seem to be needed. Then go through the revision and proofreading checklists. When you are satisfied with your description, make a final copy.

What Have You Learned in Unit 4?

Use these questions to gather and review your thoughts about the writing you did in Unit 4. Don't worry about writing complete sentences. Just put some thoughts, ideas, and reactions down for each question.

Test Essay

1. What is a test essay prompt?

_____

2. What should you look for in a test essay prompt?

_____

3. How can you quickly organize your thoughts for a test essay?

_____

4. Why should you stop drafting a few minutes before the deadline?

_____

5. Why is it a good idea to skip a line between lines of writing?

_____

Technical Description

6. What is the purpose of a technical description?

_____

7. What is one important characteristic of a technical description?

_____

8. Why is it important to keep your readers in mind when writing a technical description?

_____

9. What is the purpose of an audience needs chart for a technical description?

_____

10. Why is it important to explain technical terms?

_____

▶ If you can, share your answers with a partner or group. Share the ideas and experiences you had. Talk about problems you had while writing. Talk about your successes, too. Develop a group list of tips for each kind of writing you did in this unit.

The Writing Process

The writing process	What happens when a writer turns words into a story or an essay? He or she follows a set of steps, from start to finish. These steps make up the writing process. If you follow the same steps, you can make the process work for you.
What is a process?	A process is a series of steps that lead to a goal. Each step brings the process closer to the goal. Suppose you wanted to grow a pepper plant in a pot. Growing a plant is a process. You choose seeds, plant them, water the plants, and pull weeds. Each step gets you closer to your goal, and finally you pick the peppers.
What is the writing process?	There are five main steps in the writing process. They are prewriting, drafting, revising, proofreading, and publishing. This chart shows them. You won't always follow them in order, and you may move back and forth between stages.

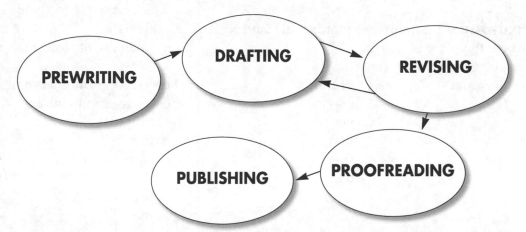

Prewriting	In prewriting, you decide what to write. This step is like deciding what seeds to grow. You explore your idea. You think about it and gather information about it. You organize your ideas. You think about the people you will be writing for. You decide what they need to know and how you want to tell it to them.
Drafting	In drafting, you put your ideas into words. You shape your words into sentences. You build your sentences into paragraphs. As you draft, you do not have to worry about parts that are not quite right. You will fix them in the next stage.
Revising	In revising, you improve your draft. You look for weak spots, such as a word that is not quite right. You make changes, or revisions, to strengthen those spots. Notice that the arrows in the drafting and revising sections can lead you back and forth. This part of the process is like watering and weeding in the growing process.
Proofreading	When you are satisfied with your revised work, you turn to proofreading. This stage is sometimes called editing. In this step, you check for and correct any errors you may have made in grammar, usage, and mechanics, including spelling.
Publishing	Finally, in the publishing stage, you make a final copy and publish it or share it with an audience.

GRAMMAR

Nouns A **noun** is the name of a person, place, or thing. A **common noun** names any person, place, or thing. A **proper noun** names a particular person, place, or thing.

Common Nouns	Proper Nouns
ballplayer	Cal Ripken
city	Los Angeles
river	Hudson River
country	Peru
street	Jackson Avenue

Pronouns **Pronouns** are words that stand for or take the place of nouns.

The subject pronouns are:

Singular	Plural
I	we
you	you
he	they
she	they
it	they

Use a **subject pronoun** as the subject of a sentence.

Incorrect
Her and Rosa will be here soon.
Revision
She and Rosa will be here soon.

Use **subject pronouns** after the linking verb *to be*.

Incorrect
The winners were Leroy and him.
Revision
The winners were Leroy and he.

The object pronouns are:

Singular	Plural
me	us
you	you
him	them
her	them
it	them

Use **object pronouns** as the direct objects of sentences. A direct object receives the action in a sentence.

Incorrect
Rosa will call Leo and I.
Revision
Rosa will call Leo and me.

Use object pronouns as objects of prepositions. The object of a preposition is a noun or pronoun at the end of a prepositional phrase. (See **Prepositions**.)

Incorrect
Selena wrote to Duane and I.
Revision
Selena wrote to Duane and me.

Possessive pronouns show ownership. The possessive pronouns are:

Singular	Plural
my	our
your	your
his	their
her	their
its	their

Verbs A **verb** is a word that shows action or the fact that something exists. Verbs change form to show time. These forms are called *tenses*.

Use **irregular verbs** correctly. Some verbs have unusual forms for showing that an action happened in the past. When in doubt, check a dictionary or ask a good editor (such as your teacher).

Incorrect
The group sung their hits.
Revision
The group sang their hits.

Adjectives An **adjective** is a word used to describe a noun or pronoun. A **proper adjective** is made from a proper noun. It names a particular person, place, or thing.

Use the correct form to compare adjectives. To compare two persons, places, or things, use the **comparative** form. Add *-er* to most short adjectives. Use *more* with longer adjectives. Use one or the other, not both.

Incorrect	Revision
more long movie	longer movie
thrillinger movie	more thrilling movie
more newer movie	newer movie

To compare more than two persons, places, or things, use the **superlative** form. Add *-est* to most short adjectives. Use *most* with longer adjectives. Use one or the other, not both.

Incorrect	Revision
most slow bus	slowest bus
comfortablest bus	most comfortable bus
most noisiest bus	noisiest bus

Some adjectives use different words for comparisons.

Examples

bad	worse	worst
good	better	best

Adverbs An **adverb** is a word that modifies a verb, an adjective, or another adverb.

Do not use an adjective when you need an adverb.

Incorrect	Revision
We did the job good.	We did the job well.
We did it quick.	We did it quickly.

Use the correct form to compare adverbs. To compare two actions, use the **comparative form**. Add *-er* to most short adverbs. Use *more* with most adverbs. Use one or the other, not both.

Incorrect	Revision
spoke more softlier	spoke more softly
started more later	started later

To compare more than two actions, use the **superlative form**. 1. Use *-est* with some short adverbs. 2. Use *most* with most adverbs. 3. Use one or the other, not both.

Incorrect	Revision
spoke most softliest	spoke most softly
started most latest	started latest

Some adverbs use different words for comparisons.

Examples

badly	worse	worst
well	better	best

Prepositions A preposition is a word that relates the noun or pronoun following it to another word in the sentence.

Examples

in	on	off	of	under
over	along	beside	above	between

I saw the funnel of a tornado in the distance. The funnel was moving in my direction.

Sentences A **sentence** is a group of words with two main parts: a complete subject and a complete predicate. Together these parts express a complete thought.

Use complete sentences, not f**ragments**. A complete sentence has a subject and a verb. A fragment is missing one of those parts. Correct a fragment by adding the missing part.

Fragment
The book written by Gary Soto.
Revision
The book was written by Gary Soto.
Fragment
Because the rain finally stopped.
Revision
We went out because the rain finally stopped.

Avoid **run-on sentences**. A run-on sentence is really more than one sentence. Correct a run-on sentence by dividing it into two (or more) sentences.

Run-on
For months I saved all the money I earned, and I never spent any of it, and finally I had enough for the class trip.
Revision
For months I saved all the money I earned. I never spent any of it. Finally I had enough for the class trip.

Subject-Verb Agreement Make the subject and verb of a sentence agree in number. To make a subject and verb agree, make sure that both are **singular** or both are **plural**. A singular subject names one person, place, or thing. A plural subject names more than one person, place, or thing.

Incorrect
Some parts is missing.
Revision
Some parts are missing.

Be careful when a **prepositional phrase** comes between the subject and the verb. The verb must agree with the subject, not with the object of the preposition.

Incorrect
One of the parts are missing.
Revision
One of the parts is missing.

The pronoun *I* is singular, but it nearly always takes the plural form of a verb. (The only exceptions are *am* and *was*, which are singular forms of the verb *to be*.)

Incorrect
I urges you to act now.
Revision
I urge you to act now.
Incorrect
I is nearly ready.
Revision
I am nearly ready.

Phrases

A **phrase** is a group of words, without a subject and verb, that works in a sentence as one part of speech.

A **prepositional phrase** is a group of words that includes a **preposition** and the **object of the preposition**, a noun or pronoun. The whole phrase works like an adjective or adverb. It modifies the meaning of another word or group of words.

Keep prepositions and their phrases close to the words they modify. Your sentence may not say what you mean if a prepositional phrase is in the wrong place.

One Meaning
The car with stripes looks great.
(but another car does not)
Another Meaning
The car looks great with stripes.
(but not without stripes)

Negatives

A **negative** is a word or word part

that means "not." The word *not* itself is a negative. So are *nobody* and *nowhere*. The contraction *-n't* is made from *not*. When *-n't* is part of a word, it is a negative.

Use only one negative in a sentence. More than one negative in a sentence is a "double negative." Remove double negatives in your sentences.

Incorrect
We don't have no blank cassettes.
Revision
We don't have any blank cassettes.
We have no blank cassettes.

MECHANICS

Capitalization

Capitalize the first word of a sentence.

Incorrect
the sun looked like an orange.
Revision
The sun looked like an orange.

Capitalize proper nouns.

Incorrect	**Revision**
boston red sox	Boston Red Sox
ernesto galarza	Ernesto Galarza
thailand	Thailand

Capitalize proper adjectives.

Incorrect
foreign and american cars
Revision
foreign and American cars

Capitalize the first word and all important words in titles of books, movies, and other works of art.

Incorrect	**Revision**
the tragedy of romeo and juliet	*The Tragedy of Romeo and Juliet*

Capitalize a person's title when it is followed by the person's name.

Incorrect	**Revision**
senator Marston	Senator Marston

Punctuation

End Marks

Use an end mark at the end of

every sentence. Use a period to end a sentence that makes a statement or gives a command. Use a question mark to end a question. Use an exclamation point after a statement showing strong emotion.

Incorrect
This is the movie to see
Have you seen it already
Yes, and it's great
Revisions
This is the movie to see.
Have you seen it already?
Yes, and it's great!

Commas Use a comma between the two independent clauses in a compound sentence.

Incorrect
Levon was standing in the doorway and his brother was sitting on the sofa.
Revision
Levon was standing in the doorway, and his brother was sitting on the sofa.

Use commas to separate three or more words in a series.

Incorrect
I bought a shirt a cap and a compact disc.
Revision
I bought a shirt, a cap, and a compact disc.

Use commas to set the rest of the sentence apart from the spoken words in a direct quotation.

Incorrect
She said "I'm not ready."
"Wait here" he said "until I return."
Revision
She said, "I'm not ready."
"Wait here," he said, "until I return."

Quotation Marks A direct quotation represents a person's exact words. Use quotation marks around the words the speaker says.

Incorrect
Mr. Hsu said, Take tomorrow off.
Revision
Mr. Hsu said, "Take tomorrow off."

When you use a comma or a period with a direct quotation, place it inside the final quotation mark.

Incorrect
"I'll see you tomorrow", I said.
She said, "I'll be waiting".
Revision
"I'll see you tomorrow," I said.
She said, "I'll be waiting."

When you use a question mark or exclamation point with a direct quotation, place it inside the quotation marks if it goes with the speaker's words.

Incorrect
I called, "Is anybody home"?
A voice answered, "I'll be right there"!
Revision
I called, "Is anybody home?"
A voice answered, "I'll be right there!"

Dialogue is written conversation. When you write dialogue, start a new paragraph each time the speaker changes. Begin a new paragraph each time a different person speaks.

Incorrect
"Good morning," he said. "Says who?" I answered.
Revision
"Good morning," he said.
"Says who?" I answered.

Apostrophes A possessive noun shows ownership, as *Luis's* does in *Luis's dog*. To make a singular noun possessive, add an apostrophe (') and an *s*, no matter what letter ends the noun.

Noun	Possessive
student	student's
boss	boss's

To make a plural noun possessive, add an apostrophe and an *s* if the noun ends with some letter other than *s*. Add only an apostrophe if the noun ends with *s*.

Noun	Possessive
children	children's
students	students'
families	families'
lawyers	lawyers'

Possessive pronouns show ownership, like possessive nouns. However, possessive pronouns are not spelled with apostrophes.

Incorrect
Those snapshots are their's.
The dog ate it's food.

Revision
Those snapshots are theirs.
The dog ate its food.

USAGE

bad, badly Use *bad* after linking verbs, such as *feel*, *look*, and *seem*. Use *badly* whenever an adverb is needed.

Incorrect
I felt badly about not being able to play in the game.

Revision
I felt bad about not being able to play in the game.

beside, besides Do not confuse these two prepositions, which have different meanings. Beside means "at the side of" or "close to." Besides means "in addition to."

Incorrect
I wondered whether anyone would be going on the trip beside the usual group.

Revision
I wondered whether anyone would be going on the trip besides the usual group.

can, may The verb *can* generally refers to the ability to do something. The verb *may* generally refers to permission to do something.

Incorrect
"Can I have the last hamburger?" he asked.

Revision
"May I have the last hamburger?" he asked.

good, well Use the predicate adjective *good* after linking verbs, such as *feel*, *look*, *smell*, *taste*, and *seem*. Use *well* whenever you need an adverb.

Incorrect
We hadn't won the game, but we could hold our heads high because we knew that we played good.

Revision
We hadn't won the game, but we could hold our heads high because we knew that we played well.

its, it's Do not confuse the possessive pronoun *its* with the contraction *it's*, standing for *it is* or *it has*.

Incorrect
That dog has something stuck in it's paw.

Revision
That dog has something stuck in its paw.

of, have Do not use *of* in place of *have* after auxiliary verbs, such as *would*, *could*, *should*, *may*, *might*, or *must*.

Incorrect
You should of seen the way Hakeem went up for the rebound.

Revision
You should have seen the way Hakeem went up for the rebound.

than, then The conjunction *than* is used to connect the two parts of a comparison. Do not confuse *than* with the adverb *then*, which usually refers to time.

Incorrect
My brother is exactly a year older then I am.

Revision
My brother is exactly a year older than I am.

their, there, they're Do not confuse the spellings of these three words. *Their* is a possessive pronoun and always modifies a noun. *There* is usually used either at the beginning of a sentence or as an adverb. *They're* is a contraction for *they are*.

Incorrect
"Are those they're sweat pants?" I asked.
"No," he said. "There over their, behind the lockers."

Revision
"Are those their sweat pants?" I asked.
"No," he said. "They're over there, behind the lockers."